Kaihan
Bizarre Crimes That Shook Japan
Vol. 1

Tara A. Devlin

Kaihan: Bizarre Crimes That Shook Japan Vol. 1
First Edition: January 2020

taraadevlin.com
© 2020 Tara A. Devlin

All rights reserved. No portion of this book may be reproduced in any form without permission from the publisher, except as permitted by U.S. copyright law.

DEDICATION

To all of you who enjoy these books. Thank you.

CONTENTS

Introduction

1 Disappearances 1

2 Robberies 83

3 Murders 95

INTRODUCTION

Before moving to Japan in the early 2000s, I used to watch a lot of news. Living in Australia, we only got the most shocking and terrifying news from faraway places such as Japan, and one of my earliest memories is of the Kobe child murders that took place in 1997. Hearing that a junior high student had beheaded a child and then left their head on a school gate was horrifying; so horrifying that I still clearly remember it over 20 years later.

When I started studying Japanese at university a few years later, I turned to watching the news in Japanese to help improve my language skills. I couldn't pick up very much, but another snippet that has always stuck with me over the years was seeing a group of police officers arguing with a man on the side of the street. The man then got into the officers' car and drove off, leaving them running down the street after him. Unlike the Kobe child murders, this was akin to watching a comedy skit on TV, and something that I often unfortunately remembered a lot when seeing actual police officers in Japan after moving there.

These two incidents sat in my mind like polar opposites, the two extremes of what Japanese crime could be. A child could be a vicious, depraved killer, or annoyed citizens could be brazen enough to jump into the patrol car of officers they were arguing with and take off, leaving them comically running behind. I've always enjoyed true crime regardless of the country, but there was something unique about the crimes taking place in Japan that always made me want to learn more.

In this book I've collected some of the most bizarre true crime stories to come out of Japan over the last few decades. From murders to robberies to disappearances, these strange incidents will leave you scratching your head and wondering "why?" or perhaps even "how?" Some of these crimes have been solved, most have not, but even for those where we know what happened, the specifics are so mind boggling that people still question them today. This is no ordinary true crime book. These are the strange, the weird, the bizarre, where little makes sense and they'll have you thinking long after you've finished reading.

I lived in Japan while several of the crimes in this book were taking place. I watched them in real time on the news and followed their development. In particular, the Shimane Female University Student Corpse Discovery is a story close to my heart because I lived in Shimane for 10 years. It wasn't just all over the news, it was all people at work talked about at the time. Shimane is a small prefecture, the second smallest in all of Japan population-wise with the highest percentage of elderly people. It's a small, rural place, so the discovery of a young university student's severed head in the mountains rocked the community. I watched the news each day waiting for the killer to be found, and my colleagues often discussed it during breaks as well. The crime was so brutal, so bizarre, and went years without any leads. In fact, it wasn't solved until several years after I left the country, and I was unaware it had even been solved until I started research for this book. The shocking truth behind the crime only made things even more bizarre, however, and even now it's still hard to believe.

But it's true.

People often say that truth is stranger than fiction. They may just be right.

As a final warning, some of the crimes mentioned in this book feature talk of subjects that some readers may find upsetting. Several of the crimes are particularly brutal, and many of the victims are women and children. If you are squeamish or uncomfortable, this may not be the book for you.

DISAPPEARANCES

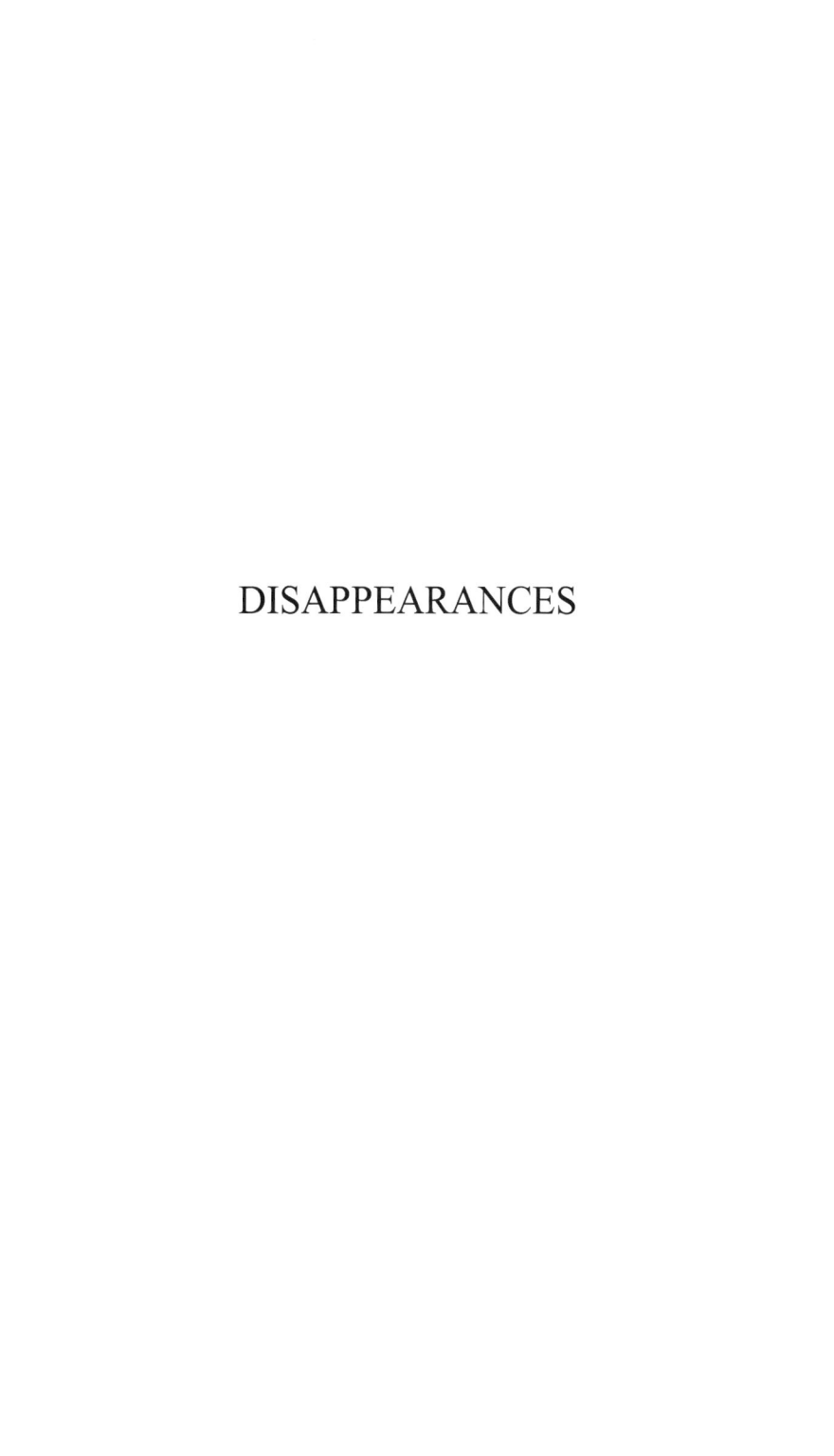

SOS Disaster Incident

Situated near the exact centre of Hokkaido you'll find Mount Asahi, the tallest mountain on the northernmost island of Japan. Coming in at 2,290.9 metres tall, Mount Asahi is an active volcano found in the Daisetsuzan mountain range that's popular with hikers during summer and skiers during winter. And in 1989, it became famous for something far more mind-boggling.

On July 24, 1989, two hikers went missing while climbing Mount Asahi. The Hokkaido police organised a search party and set out in their helicopter to find them. While in the air, the search party discovered the letters "SOS" formed by large tree trunks on the mountainside. Thinking this was a sign from the lost hikers, the search party soon found them roughly three kilometres north of the trees. Both hikers were rescued without problem thanks to the SOS sign pointing the helicopter in their direction. When the search team asked them about it, however, things suddenly took a turn for the strange.

The hikers knew nothing of any SOS sign.

The two men had made a simple yet common mistake whilst hiking. There is a large rock called Kinko Iwa near the peak of Mount Asahi, so named because of its resemblance to a *kinko*, or safe, that many people use as a landmark when hiking. There is, however, a "fake" Kinko Iwa as well; another rock that looks similar to the real thing, but if used as a landmark, leads people in the wrong direction instead. This fake Kinko Iwa has led many a hiker astray, and the terrain quickly becomes treacherous when heading the wrong way. The hiking path gives way to sheer cliffs and copious bamboo grass; it's easy enough to go down, but when you realise you've gone the wrong way, it's suddenly impossible to get back up.

In this instance, the hikers were saved without problem, all thanks to that giant SOS sign on the side of the mountain. But, if they hadn't created it, then who had?

The search party realised that there had to be another person lost on the mountain. The following day they began their search again, this time finding human skeletal remains close to the sign. This was where things got even weirder.

Asahikawa Medical University conducted testing on the bone fragment the search party had found. The bone showed evidence of an animal bite, meaning the person had likely been mauled to death. The items discovered by the remains were crosschecked with missing person's lists and it was determined that they belonged to a 25-year-old businessman from Aichi Prefecture who went missing in 1985, four years earlier.

But things got even stranger still. Testing determined the bones to be female, yet no feminine items were recovered from the rescue site, and a cassette tape found by the body featured a male voice calling for help. No matter how they looked at it, the victim was clearly a male, yet the tests determined the bones to be female. It threw both the police and the media into a frenzy. The contents of the cassette tape didn't help, either. The man recorded over one section of the tape, originally a collection of anime theme songs. The transcript of that recording went as follows:

"I'm on a cliff and can't move. S O S. Help me. I'm on a cliff and can't move. S O S. Help me. I'm at the spot where I first saw the helicopter. The bamboo grass is too deep and I can't go anywhere. Please lift me up from here."

The entire recording lasted two minutes and 17 seconds and posed more questions than it answered. First of all, why did the victim make the recording in the first place? The man screamed each syllable loudly and clearly, punctuated with a brief pause between each sound. He was healthy and energetic enough at this point to yell, but why did he record it? What good would that do?

Some have suggested that perhaps he recorded the call for help so he could play it when he was no longer strong enough to use his own voice, but considering the technology of the time, even screaming at full volume wasn't likely to reach anyone's ears. Others have suggested that the tape was in his bag when he saw a helicopter passing by and he somehow pressed record while yelling for it. This also seems unlikely, as there was no background noise and the man spoke clearly into the recorder, not through the material of a bag.

To date, nobody knows why he made the recording. Even stranger, the man's body was found in wetlands with no cliffs around. Where was this cliff he spoke of? If he was—as he proclaimed in his recording—stuck on a cliff and unable to move, why was his body found in wetlands with plenty of room to move around and not a cliff in sight?

Perhaps the biggest mystery, however, lay in the SOS sign itself. The sign was made using Japanese white birch tree trunks. It measured roughly three metres in height and five metres in length, with numerous trunks gathered and laid out to spell the three letters. The tree trunks were heavy, and to manoeuvre them all into place would have taken a great deal of energy and strength. Assuming the man was strong enough to move them all alone, why didn't he use that energy to escape instead? And putting that aside, how did the trees last five years on the mountainside before anyone ever saw them? The trunks were cleaned up a few months later by the police, but their existence remained wrapped in mystery.

One mystery *was* eventually solved regarding this strange incident; the victim's bones were retested a few days after the original test (and media confusion) and this time proven to be male, not female. A mistake had been made somewhere in the original testing process, quickly bringing that particular part of the investigation to a close. The other mysteries, to this date, have yet to be solved.

In 1984, a single hiker went missing on his trip to Hokkaido from Aichi. He created an SOS sign out of large tree trunks, recorded his call for help, but unfortunately wasn't found in time. A wild animal likely dealt his death blow, and he remained officially missing until five years later when two separate hikers got lost in the same area. These hikers were discovered and saved, perhaps ironically, thanks to his sign. Why did he record his screams for help over an anime theme song tape? How was he strong enough to move so many large tree trunks into place? Why did he proclaim to be stuck on a cliff when his body was found in an open area with no cliffs in sight?

It is perhaps a bittersweet irony that the man's monumental efforts did nothing to save himself, but did lead to the rescue of two other lives half a decade later. His own death, however, remains a mystery that boggles the mind to this day.

Muroran Female High School Student Disappearance

On March 6, 2001, 16-year-old Chida Asami called the bakery she worked at part-time to inform them she would be in soon to take a coffee-making course. A brilliant student from the nearby Hokkaido Muroransakae High School, Chida had the day off thanks to entrance exams taking place at school that same day.

It was a Tuesday. Chida was in the apartment she shared with her parents and younger brother in Hakuchodai, roughly seven kilometres from the bakery in Nakajimacho. Chida normally worked at the branch store across the road from her apartment, but friends claimed she wanted to work at the bakery's head branch which was closer to school and thus more convenient for her to reach after. She hoped that taking the coffee course at the head store would help her do that.

A female employee of the head bakery answered Chida's call around 11:30 a.m. Chida explained she would be at the store sometime around 1 p.m. that day and asked if the owner was in. He wasn't at the time, but he *would* come in to see her. Chida then hung up and set out to reach the bakery. Her actions immediately following this call proved confusing, however, and to this day still haven't been explained.

There was a bus stop directly in front of Chida's apartment, yet rather than getting on the bus here, Chida walked all the way to a further stop and got on there instead. Being a day off, Chida was not in her school uniform, but rather dressed in jeans, a beige blazer, Burberry scarf, and green leather shoes. She looked like any other regular woman heading out for the day; meaning she blended into the crowd more easily than if she had been in school uniform.

After stopping at a convenience store, Chida got on the bus at Hakuchodai Central around 12:25 p.m. Here a friend saw her, and Chida waved to her from the back of the bus. The bus was heading for Higashimachi Terminal, a bus stop outside Chida's high school. At 12:56 p.m., the bus stopped at Higashidoori, the bus stop immediately next to the bakery. This had Chida right on time for her scheduled 1 p.m. arrival, and yet, she didn't get off the bus.

Chida eventually got off three stops later, sometime after 1 p.m. She entered the nearby Muroran Saty mall and was seen on security cameras browsing makeup from 1:04 to 1:26 p.m. She showed no signs of being in a rush; on the contrary, she appeared relaxed and took her time looking through items and exploring the store. Chida's appointment at the bakery was 1 p.m. The bus she took got her there on time, and yet she went right past it and took her time browsing the nearby mall instead. Why?

After leaving the mall, Chida was spotted by two male classmates. They waved at her from across the road and she waved back. Chida got back on the bus heading towards the bakery at 1:31 p.m., and it's believed she got off at Higashidoori at the scheduled 1:41 p.m. stop. It's believed because nobody knows for certain. Her two classmates were the last people known to have seen her in public.

At 1:42 p.m., immediately after Chida got off the bus, she received a call from her boyfriend on her PHS (personal handy-phone system, a type of cordless telephone that works well in dense urban areas with many receivers, but less so in rural areas with fewer receivers). She informed him that she'd just arrived at "Shimo," local slang for the downtown area the bakery was in. It's important to note at this point that the bus stop was literally next door to the bakery, barely 10 metres away from the shop's entrance. Her boyfriend called her again four minutes later, but this time Chida informed him, "I can't talk right now, so I'll call you back." This was the last anyone ever heard of her.

The calls made to Chida's PHS confirmed she was in the area at the time, although they could not pinpoint an exact location. The receiver box for the PHS when she got the calls sat above the bus stop, meaning she was within a 100 metre radius of it at the time. Yet instead of entering the bakery, just a few short metres away, Chida seemingly disappeared off the face of the earth instead.

So, what happened? Was Chida murdered? Abducted? How could her disappearance be reconciled with her strange behaviour beforehand?

Chida was a grade A student. Muroransakae High School was one of the best in the area, often sending its students to top-class universities, and Chida was considered one of the best students there. Not only was she intelligent, but she was both pretty and popular, with numerous male admirers and, apparently, even a stalker. Chida had revealed to both her branch manager and head bakery owner that she was having troubles with an unwanted admirer, but because this was taking place mostly over text messages and phone calls, she herself wasn't hugely concerned by it. Yet the fact remained that Chida was popular. Very popular.

When Chida's boyfriend tried calling her again, he was unable to get through to her PHS. According to the bakery owner, he went home at 1:30 p.m. after Chida hadn't shown up, claiming he felt "unwell." When Chida didn't arrive home that night, her parents grew worried and contacted the police. The police were slow to respond, however, and many have criticised them over the years for this fact, blaming them for botching the investigation and potentially letting the criminal slip through their fingers.

In most missing person cases, the police use sniffer dogs in an attempt to locate the missing person. Yet the police carried out no such search for Chida, and angry outcries from the public have accused them of not treating the initial case seriously. Because Chida was a high school girl, perhaps they thought that "teenagers often do this sort of thing" and she would return on her own. Had the police taken the sniffer dogs out to find her right away, the chance of locating her would have been much higher. Yet they did nothing, and the trail immediately went cold.

It wasn't until March 18, two weeks later, that the police officially announced Chida's disappearance. One week after that, on March 24, they distributed thousands of missing person leaflets throughout the city, yet they were again criticised for the small number of leaflets they handed out. During this time they also investigated those closest to Chida, and one person in particular stood out as a suspect: the head bakery owner, the man Chida was going to meet.

The baker owner was suspicious for several reasons. First, he had no alibi for Chida's time of disappearance. By his own admission, he left the bakery at 1:30 p.m. after Chida didn't show up for her 1 p.m. appointment. He claimed he "wasn't feeling well" and went home to sleep. Investigations revealed that the man owned not just the bakery, but the entire building the bakery was located in; the first floor held the bakery front and kitchen, while the second and third floors each held three rental apartments apiece. Of those, two were empty. A small parking lot in the rear of the building was also largely secluded from the public and difficult to see from the street.

One possibility considered was that the owner had kidnapped Chida and hidden her in one of the empty rooms above the bakery before moving her elsewhere. Police held and questioned the owner for three days, searching both his private home and businesses, but they couldn't find a single thing linking him to the disappearance. In the end he was released without charge, but the police kept him in their sights.

One year later, the owner closed the bakery and moved to a new area before filing for bankruptcy. The building in question was auctioned and sold to a new owner, and the former owner's private residence was demolished. Not only was the house demolished, but the former owner called in heavy machinery to dig up the foundations. Was Chida buried beneath the house? No evidence was ever unearthed, but the owner remained high on the police's suspect list. In fact, he was generally considered to be the only real suspect. But that didn't mean there weren't others.

Chida's boyfriend was also briefly considered. The timing of his call right as Chida got off the bus, and then again a few minutes later, moments before she disappeared, seemed almost *too* convenient. Like he was trying to create an alibi for himself. In addition, few people in Chida's circle of friends knew of his existence. Why did she keep him a secret from them? Yet this line of reasoning also went nowhere, as there was no evidence of any wrongdoing on the man's part, only the suspicious timing of his calls.

With the bakery owner and Chida's boyfriend ruled out due to lack of evidence, the police were not only at a loss, they found themselves confronted with all sorts of contradictory information. Chida started working part time at the bakery's branch store in December 2000. She'd only been working there four months at the time of her disappearance. According to staff who worked there at the time, the bakery had no "coffee course." If no such course existed, why was Chida heading to work in the first place? Why did the owner agree to meet her for a course that didn't exist? And why did she overshoot her bus stop, spend time walking around a nearby mall, and then return over 40 minutes later before disappearing into thin air?

Another point of confusion was Chida's last call to her boyfriend. She told him that she couldn't talk at that moment and would call him back. Her boyfriend claimed that it sounded like she was inside a building. That it was quiet. At the time, construction was taking place on the building opposite the bakery, with many large trucks coming and going all day, in addition to the usual noise of construction work. This should have been picked up on the call if she was outside, but he claimed to hear nothing. In the three minutes after his first call to her, Chida had moved somewhere quiet enough that the sounds of nearby construction were drowned out. She didn't enter the bakery; none of the staff saw her in the front nor in the kitchen. The majority of nearby buildings were private apartments, and she was not captured on the security cameras of any stores. So, where was she?

The media claimed that Chida disappeared in broad daylight from a busy public area, but this was not true. While the bus stop was on was a main thoroughfare, the rest of the area was full of small side streets that saw little human traffic. The local hospital was also just a few streets away, behind which lay a massive forest; the perfect place to disappear in. Police *did* search the forest, but they found no sign of Chida's body, nor that she had been there to begin with.

With construction taking place across the road, numerous large trucks were coming and going all day, in addition to delivery vehicles for the bakery (which may or may not have used the hidden car park to the rear of the building). Any of these vehicles could have potentially abducted Chida and ferried her out of sight before anyone realised. Everything had to be considered.

Another theory proposed that Chida faked her own disappearance. Although she got good grades and went to one of the best schools in the area, it was said that Chida had no ambitions of entering a top level university; rather, she wanted to enter nursing school. It was suggested that perhaps her parents had other wishes and were pressuring her, although there was never any proof of this. On the contrary, the Chida family appeared to get along quite well. Yet there were also (unsubstantiated) rumours that they may have been having money troubles, and that the reason Chida even began her bakery job—according to the theory—was to save money so she could run away. And yet no proof was ever discovered of the family having money troubles.

Friends also claimed that Chida was a methodical notebook keeper. At the time of her disappearance, her notebook was still in the house. Suspiciously, it disappeared soon thereafter. Yet there was no sign that Chida was depressed or troubled, nor was there any real evidence to suggest that she had been planning to make herself disappear due to family troubles, financial troubles, or otherwise.

Yet another possibility was that North Koreans had abducted her. She wouldn't have been the first person abducted from Hokkaido, nor the first to have been snatched in broad daylight from a public area. Eyewitness reports placed a person who looked similar to Chida at Itanki Beach (a few kilometres away) the very next day, lending more support to the theory. The Japanese government currently only recognises 17 abductions of Japanese citizens by North Korea, but the National Police Agency claims that the real number could be as high as 879. People targeted for abduction were often young and female. Could Chida be amongst the numerous potential abductees? Nobody knows for sure. There are too many strange elements regarding her case that confuse matters.

With a lack of evidence as to her whereabouts, it didn't take long for outlandish rumours to start spreading. One story claimed that Chida's body was disposed of in Horobetsu Dam, roughly 10 kilometres away. Others claimed to see her hanging around local parks. Others said she'd taken on a new name and was living in a different city. Another story claimed that the bakery branch owner—the store across the road from Chida's house—committed suicide after her disappearance, possibly implicating him in it. Yet none of these rumours were ever substantiated, and to this day, nobody knows what happened to her.

You can still find missing person's posters for Chida around the area she disappeared, and officially, the case remains open.

Shouyama Jin Disappearance

Sunday. February 23, 1969. 14-year-old Shouyama Jin from Sasebo City in Nagasaki Prefecture was working on some crafts for school on the veranda of his family home when he grabbed his school hat and told his parents he was heading out. It was just after 2 p.m. and he left his tools as-is on the veranda. Wearing his school uniform, Shouyama left the house to head into town. His family never saw him again.

Around 6 p.m. that same day, a 24-year-old man showed up to the Shouyama household holding Jin's hat. "The owner of this hat stole my money," he told them. He then went on to elaborate:

"I was on a road in the city around 3:30 p.m. A bike had fallen into a ditch, and I tried to help two boys out of it. I took my jumper off and placed it on the side of the road to help them. One of the boys suddenly grabbed my jumper and ran, and then the junior high student followed him. There was 460,000 yen in that jumper pocket. I chased after the junior high student and grabbed this hat out of his back pocket, but the two of them got away. I found you by relying on the name written in the hat."

Shouyama's family were shocked. This sounded nothing like their son at all, and they had no idea who this stranger holding his hat was. But things were about to get even stranger. The very next day, Shouyama's father received a letter addressed to him at lunchtime. It was from his son.

Dispensing with preliminaries,

I'm sorry for worrying you. One of my bad friends made me steal the money. There was more than 400,000 yen in there, but I only received a little. Please tell school that I'll be absent for a while until I sort myself out. I'll return home soon and apologise.

Please don't come looking for me.
Jin.

The handwriting was Shouyama's, but it appeared he had been forced and not written it of his own free will. Either way, the note was unsettling.

At this point, Shouyama's parents were only certain of one thing; he had left home at 2 p.m. the day before wearing his school uniform and hat, and he had yet to return home. It may seem odd for a 14-year-old boy to be wearing a school uniform on a Sunday, but at the time it wasn't that uncommon. Now, a man was claiming that their son had stolen a large amount of money from him, and a letter written by Jin's hand seemed to confirm that story. Yet things didn't add up. Something about the situation seemed wrong.

The Shouyama family went to the police, and the police agreed the situation didn't seem right. They immediately turned their sights to the 24-year-old man with Shouyama's hat. Although he worked in a cleaning store at the time, it turned out that he had been released on parole from a two-year stint in juvenile prison only four months earlier. The authenticity of the man's story quickly came into question, and several doubts were raised.

First, where did the man get this supposed money from? He had only been released from prison four months earlier, and 400,000 yen (roughly $4000) was hardly chump change at the time. He worked as a cleaner—not exactly the highest paying job around—meaning it would be near impossible to save that much money in such a short amount of time. He also claimed that he had hidden the money under the floor at his family home, but his family claimed to have no knowledge of any such money.

Second, there were no witnesses to the incident he described. The man claimed that the boys stole his jumper around 3:30 p.m. in broad daylight from a city street. Yet nobody saw any of them, and investigations revealed no bike tracks in the gutter where the man claimed the incident took place. Moreover, it was a Sunday, meaning the banks weren't open, putting why the man had so much money in his pocket into even more question. Plus, how did the boys know the money was in there in the first place? It seemed strange to police that two young boys would go to all that trouble just to steal a man's jumper, not knowing that anything might be inside it at the time.

Third, the use of the phrase "*dispensing with preliminaries*" in Shouyama's letter sounded odd and forced. The boy had never used the phrase before, and even wrote his own name wrong, suggesting that he was being coerced and perhaps even threatened at the time. The police drew their own conclusions, thinking it likely that Shouyama had actually been kidnapped, and that the man who had come to his house holding his hat was attempting to ransom the "stolen money" from his parents. The day after Shouyama disappeared, the police organised a large-scale search of the surrounding mountains for him. However, they found nothing.

On February 25, two days after his disappearance, the police officially opened their investigation into Shouyama's whereabouts. They pursued the man, identified as A, as the main suspect, even hooking him up to a lie detector machine during questioning, but were unable to pin anything on him. The theory was that A, for some unknown reason, kidnapped the boy, took him somewhere secret, forced him to write the letter, and then appeared before his parents to get the imaginary stolen money back. But all of this seemed difficult for a single person to carry out alone, and investigations revealed that he may have had accomplices.

Before showing up at Shouyama's house, A had been seen around town asking where the family lived. Yet 30 minutes before that, a group of three different men had also been asking people around town the same question. Who were they, and why did they also want to know where the family lived? It was too much to simply be a coincidence, but the police were unable to discover who the men were. It was possible that they were friends of A's from prison, but without any solid leads, the men's identities remained a mystery.

In the end, the police were unable to turn up anything about Shouyama's whereabouts. It seemed likely that when the boy's parents went to the police, rather than paying A back the "stolen" money, the boy was killed and his body buried out of sight. But with no body, no proof, and no leads, the case went nowhere, and to this day remains unsolved.

A year after his disappearance, Shouyama's family moved to Saga Prefecture, and not long after the investigation began, A moved as well, leaving Sasebo behind and moving from city to city before eventually settling in Nara Prefecture. A reporter visited him several years after the fact to ask him questions about the case, which ended up raising even more questions.

When asked about the origin of the money, A claimed that it wasn't illicit, and although he still couldn't say how he got it right then and there, he would "probably have to say it someday." Why he couldn't reveal how he got the money at that moment, but felt that someday he would have to come clean about it, was unclear. When questioned about how it was strange for the boys to notice the money in his jumper, the man said, "Yeah. You couldn't see it from the outside. Come to think of it, that is strange." Strange indeed.

Even more befuddling was when the reporter asked A about Shouyama's height. A reportedly jolted, perhaps not expecting to be asked such a question, and answered, "About the same size as me, or maybe a little taller." A, according to the reporter, was a short and stout man. Shouyama, on the other hand, was tall for his age, already reaching 168 centimetres at 14; meaning Shouyama would have towered over him. How could A not know how tall the boy was? According to his own story, he chased after Shouyama and got close enough to grab his hat out of his back pocket. This would have been more than enough to realise how tall the boy was, yet the question threw him and he gave a wrong answer.

It begged the question, if A didn't know how tall Shouyama was, then had he ever even seen him? Were the three men asking around town for his address the real perpetrators? Was A just helping them on the side? Did the men—perhaps former prison mates—meet with him one day, reveal that they planned to kidnap and ransom a boy back to his family under the pretence of "stolen" money, and rope him in to do the face-to-face work? After all, if he never had any contact with the boy and investigations turned to him, they wouldn't be able to find anything incriminating. And it was true, the lie detector test didn't find anything, perhaps because A really wasn't involved in his disappearance… not directly, anyway.

To this day, all we have are theories. Shouyama was never found and nobody was ever charged for his disappearance. Numerous details about his case didn't add up, and while the working theory was that he was kidnapped and then probably killed, without a body and without evidence, it was all just that; a theory.

Tabata Sakunosuke Hit & Run

At 4:30 p.m. on March 3, 1978, the day of the Hina Matsuri holiday, 3-year-old Tabata Sakunosuke was playing on the road outside his home in Osaka with another boy from the neighbourhood. A car driving down the street suddenly ran into Sakunosuke, knocking the boy to the ground. The other boy, 5-years-old, reported that Sakunosuke lay still and blood poured from his head as the driver stopped and got out of his car.

"Whose child is this?" the man asked, looking down at him. He then continued. "There's no time to wait for the ambulance, so I'll take him to the hospital myself." The man bundled the bleeding boy into his car and took off. He was never seen again.

The neighbourhood boy quickly ran to Sakunosuke's house and informed his mother of what happened. They both rushed back outside, but the driver and Sakunosuke were gone. Sakunosuke's mother then called nearby hospitals to see if her son had been admitted to any, but none had seen him. Finding this highly suspicious, she then went to the police, and the following day they began looking into the incident as a kidnapping.

The neighbourhood boy wasn't the only witness to the crime. A female teacher had been passing on her bike at the time, and a labourer from a nearby construction site were amongst several adults who also saw the hit and run.

The March 5 edition of the *Asahi Newspaper* reported on the incident and revealed the police had put together a montage photo of the man they were looking for in connection to the kidnapping. He was said to be in his 40s, not wearing a suit, and driving a white car (potentially a Toyota Corolla) which was heading south as it fled the scene of the crime.

Eyewitness reports said the driver didn't stop until he was at least 10 or 20 metres away. The police also found no evidence that the car had suddenly slammed on the brakes, leading them to believe that the driver hadn't been looking when he hit Sakunosuke, or had perhaps intended to hit him. This, combined with the man bundling the child into his car and disappearing led to suspicions that he may have been drunk driving at the time. It was the end of the work day on a Friday. The man was not in a suit. Eyewitnesses claimed the man sounded oddly calm when he picked the boy up and put him in his car, not panicked like one might imagine after suddenly hitting a child. Was it alcohol? Drugs? Or did he have his sights set on the boy and planned to kidnap him all along…?

One popular theory is that the man wasn't trying to kidnap Sakunosuke; he was merely trying to hide his crime. 2018 saw 3,532 traffic-related deaths in Japan, but in 1978, that number was 8,466. Drink driving was more common, speeding was more common, and as a result, traffic-related deaths were much higher. Greater public education and stiffer laws over the years have seen the number of deaths decrease, but when Sakunosuke was hit, it wasn't uncommon for people to drink, drive, and then speed home while still intoxicated. Numerous drivers questioned about hit and runs over the years have all said the same thing; they ran because they were scared. They didn't want to get caught. It's thought that when the man—potentially drunk and not thinking straight—saw that he'd hit a young boy who was now bleeding and unmoving, he put him in his car to hide the evidence. He then sped off, and neither of them were seen again.

Sakunosuke's family lived near the Hanshin Expressway No. 15 Sakai Route. This meant their neighbourhood saw little traffic during the day, making it a safe place for children to play, but when rush hour came, many cars left the congested highway and used their side street as a detour. The expressway also had a toll which some drivers avoided by turning off and taking the local streets. It's likely, considering the day and time that Sakunosuke was hit, that the driver was one of those cars looking to avoid the congested expressway.

None of the witnesses caught the number plate as the car drove away, and it was a time before security cameras on the streets were common. With little information to go on, the police struggled to get anywhere with the case, and on March 3, 1983, the statute of limitations on both kidnapping and criminal negligence leading to injury passed. By this time, Sakunosuke would have been 8-years-old if still alive, but that was perhaps the hardest part for his family to bear. Nobody knew whether the boy was still alive, perhaps being raised by his kidnapper, or whether the boy had died and the man dumped his body somewhere yet to be found.

If still alive, Sakunosuke would be in his 40s today, and considering his age at the time of the accident, with little (if any) memory of what happened. Some have suggested that he may still be alive today, living under a different name with no knowledge that he was hit by a car and then kidnapped, but most agree it's more likely that the boy died of his injuries and his body was then disposed of.

As for the driver, he would be well into his 80s if still alive today. Whether he intended to hit Sakunosuke and kidnap him, or was drunk driving and took the boy to hide this fact, nobody knows, and we likely never will.

Mysterious Note Incident

On September 2, 1994, housewife Arashi Mayumi disappeared. "I'm going to meet a classmate," she said to her older sister as she left the house, leaving her one-year-old daughter behind. Mayumi was briefly living at home with her parents and older sister due to some minor complications after the birth of her child. By the next morning, however, she hadn't returned, and her family would never see her again.

People go missing in Japan all the time. Sometimes they're found within a few days, sometimes they return of their own free will, and sometimes the cases are never solved. The reason this case became famous, however, was because of a single handwritten note. That note turned an ordinary disappearance into a countrywide sensation.

On October 13, 2011, 17 years after her disappearance, Mayumi's family appeared on a television program called *Super J Channel Tsuiseki Shinjitsu no Yukue*. The program was one of many that aimed to bring light to various strange cases over the years. Program staff interviewed Mayumi's family about the lead up to her disappearance, with each giving their account of what happened. But that wasn't what caught people's attention. In the background of Mayumi's father's interview, just behind his head, was a note stuck to a bookshelf:

"Yoko no hanashi wa shinjiru na."
Don't believe Yoko's story.

This note was never referenced by the family nor the staff and it quickly piqued viewers' interests. Why was it there? Who was Yoko and what was her story? Was the family trying to tell the public something? Did the program staff realise it was there or did it slip by during the editing process?

Viewers quickly took to the 2chan bulletin boards to post about it while the program was still on the air. One poster wrote, "Behind the father there's a note that says 'Don't believe Yoko's story,'" but what's that about?" Another poster replied, "Isn't Yoko her older sister?"

And this was where things got even stranger. Arashi Mayumi had an older sister named Yoko. Yoko was the last person she spoke to before leaving on the day she disappeared. What was really going on?

The day after Mayumi went missing, her older sister went to visit the classmate she was supposed to have met. According to that classmate, however, they had never arranged a get together. Mayumi's father also noted that she seemed uneasy that day; nervous and unable to calm down. If Mayumi hadn't gone to see her classmate, then where did she go?

Don't believe Yoko's story. Yoko appeared on the program before her father to give her version of events. Eagle-eyed viewers spotted an elderly woman in the background sticking up a piece of paper behind her, most likely her mother. It appeared that Yoko herself was unaware of the note, but it was there for all to see when her father did his interview. The mystery deepened. Were her parents trying to tell the public something? What did they know, and why were they resorting to such measures to get it across? Viewers were disturbed by the potential hidden meanings in both the gesture and the note.

A simple program about a young mother's disappearance had quickly become an incident in and of itself, and the more people dug into the incident, the more it looked like Yoko may have had something to do with her sister's disappearance.

According to Yoko, and the story her parents said we shouldn't believe, she visited Mayumi's classmate the day after she disappeared and discovered that they had no such agreement to meet. That same night, however, Yoko's parents received a phone call from a mysterious man asking for her. The day after that, Yoko supposedly found a note in her clothes dresser that appeared to have been written by Mayumi. In it, Mayumi (supposedly) claimed to have been cheating on her husband with a man known as A and apologised for her actions. A's phone number was written at the bottom of the note. That night, A called Yoko several times. He then claimed that he had been with Mayumi before she disappeared. According to another mutual acquaintance of both Mayumi and Yoko's, Mayumi was supposedly spending a lot of money on A, maybe even supporting him financially, despite the fact he was also a married man.

Both the police and *Super J Channel* investigations relied largely upon Yoko's testimony. It should be noted that Yoko was the only person who could "verify" any of these claims. Nobody else saw the note Mayumi supposedly wrote because Yoko tore it up, and all the information about Mayumi's classmate and her supposed affair with A also came from her. The entire investigation was built around Yoko's claims because there was no other information.

Mayumi's parents doted on her, perhaps more so than they did with Yoko, the eldest sister. Yoko was said to be extremely jealous of that and grew even more so after the birth of Mayumi's child. In hindsight, many of Yoko's actions and claims seemed suspicious. And, if the note warning people not to believe her was anything to go by, her parents agreed.

Numerous questions are raised when looking closely at the case. The first is the note Yoko found in her drawer. This note, which only Yoko saw, supposedly featured Mayumi's confession of cheating on her husband and the phone number of A, the man she was supposedly cheating with. The most obvious question is why would Yoko throw this key piece of evidence away if it were real and not hand it over to investigators.

The second is why Mayumi—if she really did write such a note—would include the phone number of the man she was cheating with at the bottom. What would this achieve? Looking at it from Mayumi's point of view, it doesn't make sense. There's no reason for her to write this man's phone number. Looking at it from Yoko's point of view, however, there's a very good reason for including the man's number; now Yoko has a "legitimate" reason to be in contact with the man. Why would she need that? That's a good question.

Not long after Mayumi's disappearance and the discovery of the note, Yoko hired a private investigator to follow A. Yoko and A had spoken on the phone—about what, nobody knows, but with his number written on the note they now had a legitimate contact method. This private investigator, however, spent six months following A's every move, trying to catch him doing something suspicious. Private investigator's aren't cheap, but if you're trying to prove that you did nothing wrong, hiring one to follow another suspect is a good place to start.

At one point, the investigator saw A walk into a hiking trail in the mountains late at night holding two bottles of juice. This struck the investigator as suspicious; why would a man need two bottles, one in each hand, as he walked deep into the mountains? And so late at night, no less. Was it, perhaps, to take to someone he was holding captive? This might seem like sloppy behaviour from a potential criminal, but the police were called and they investigated the area. They found nothing.

One theory is that A knew he was being followed. That was why he carried two juice bottles so openly. He wanted the investigator to see. He wanted the investigator to find this suspicious. If Yoko and A were working together, this situation suddenly seems less strange. They were deliberately trying to throw people off the scent, to make A seem like the kidnapper. Why? What would A stand to gain from this? That remains unknown, but if we suppose that Yoko played a part in her sister's disappearance and then hired A to "take the fall" knowing that no evidence could be traced to him (because he didn't do anything) then she could divert attention away from herself. If all this is true, then it worked.

At least, until the note behind her father's head on national TV.

This note has posed numerous questions over the years as well. Most people agree that it's unlikely the note slipped by without the program's staff noticing it. It was too prominent, and viewers noted that the father was framed so that his head didn't obscure the note in the background; this was done on purpose. There was no way the staff weren't aware of it. But the biggest question remains: why was it there?

Yoko's parents have never publicly spoken against their daughter. This is important to keep in mind. They've never once said anything to suggest that they suspect their eldest daughter had anything to do with the disappearance of their youngest. The only clue the public had on their feelings towards the case was that note. Perhaps the parents were too frightened to speak up in front of their daughter. If they knew, or suspected, what really happened, they might have a good reason for this. Considering the police had zero evidence suggesting Yoko had anything to do with the disappearance as well, little would come out of her parents accusing her of something they couldn't prove. It would merely tear their family apart even more.

But if they wanted people to know of their suspicions, if they wanted the public to dig further into a case that was otherwise unremarkable, that mysterious note was a good way to go about it. Viewers discussing the show on 2chan after the fact suggested that Yoko's parents may not have been able to speak up vocally because they were afraid of their daughter, and with Yoko sitting just outside the room as her parents were being interviewed, she could hear everything they were saying. They couldn't outright accuse her.

Yoko's mother was seen putting the note up during her interview, just before her father's. The staff undoubtedly noticed the note and may have even asked them to take it down, but the parents—being unable to vocalise what they truly wanted to say—perhaps begged them to keep it there. The interview proceeded as normal, but what they really wanted was for people to notice the note. To start digging. To find all the inconsistencies in Mayumi's case and realise that what Yoko claimed didn't add up. They, fearing for their lives, could do nothing about it, but maybe other people could.

Mayumi's case took another baffling turn in 2013 when Yoko herself then went missing. Her family submitted a missing person's report to the police, but little information has been released to the public since. First Mayumi, and then almost 20 years later, her older sister. The woman most had come to suspect played a key role in her disappearance. The Arashis had lost both their daughters to mysterious circumstances.

Since Yoko's disappearance, no further information has been revealed to the public about either sister. The statute of limitations on Mayumi's disappearance has passed, but we're still no closer to understanding what happened. Eagle-eyed internet sleuths discovered that in 2015, Mayumi was removed from the Missing Person Search website, a database of people missing from all over Japan. Her photo and information were removed and replaced with a message stating "Thank you for your cooperation." This appears to be the standard message whenever a missing person is removed from the site, but no reason was given as to why. Was Mayumi (or her body) found? It's unlikely she was removed because her case was too old; there are still numerous missing people on the website that have been missing since the 1980s. Was her case solved, or did her parents request Mayumi's removal for their own reasons? We may never know.

Like most of the missing person cases in this book, we're unlikely to ever find out what happened to Mayumi, and later, to her sister Yoko. Numerous questions remain, and the true motives behind puzzling note that kicked all of this off remain unknown to this day.

Akagi Shrine Housewife Disappearance

Akagi Shrine in Gunma Prefecture is famous for its azalea flowers. People visit from all over Japan to see them when they're in full bloom, and it's a popular sightseeing spot throughout the year. In the late 1990s, however, it also became famous for something else; *kamikakushi*, or spiriting away.

On May 3, 1998, Shizuka Noriko, a housewife from Chiba Prefecture, got in the car with her husband, daughter, grandchild, aunt, uncle, and mother-in-law. Although the weather looked foreboding, they drove all the way from Chiba to see the famous flowers. By the time they arrived at 11:30 a.m., however, the weather had taken a turn for a worse and they found themselves in a heavy downpour.

Having driven all that way, Shizuka's husband and uncle decided to get out and pay homage at the shrine before returning home so the trip wasn't a waste. Everybody else waited in the car. As the clock approached midday, Shizuka then told those waiting with her that she was going to get out and donate some money to the shrine. She took 101 yen from her purse and stepped out into the pouring rain. She was wearing a pink long-sleeved shirt, black skirt, blue sandals with a hibiscus print, and took with her a bright red umbrella, so even amongst the heavy rain she stood out.

Shizuka made her way towards the shrine grounds, but when her daughter turned around to look at her, she saw her mother facing a different direction away from the shrine. Her mother stood still in the rain, like she was frozen, only 100 metres from the car. Her daughter found this strange and wondered what she was doing, but turned back to face the front. When she looked again only 10 seconds later, her mother was gone, as though she had vanished into thin air. As though she had been spirited away.

The term *kamikakushi* literally means to be hidden by a god. This refers to an old belief that if one angered a god, they would kidnap that person and hide them from the world; they would be spirited away and never seen again. While not many people nowadays believe that angered gods will kidnap those who upset them, the term is still widely used for people who mysteriously disappear. Shizuka had been standing on the edge of the shrine grounds in the pouring rain, staring at something unseen in the opposite direction. Her daughter turned away for only a few moments, but when she looked back, she was gone. It was the epitome of *kamikakushi*, and it was a term the media ran with when reporting on her mysterious disappearance.

Shizuka was 48-years-old, 156 centimetres tall, and described as slightly chubby. She wore hearing aids in daily life and was said to get dizzy if she didn't wear them. She had been known, on occasion, to fall over from this dizziness, and when she stepped out of the car to enter Akagi Shrine, she wasn't wearing her aids. Clearly she didn't intend to go very far, because without them she would suffer from dizzy spells, and she left both her bag and wallet in the car. So, where did she go?

When Shizuka's husband and uncle returned to the car, they learnt that she had left to visit the shrine as well. They remarked that they hadn't seen her, which was strange, because they would have if she'd entered the shrine grounds. The Golden Week holidays were in full swing, meaning people were visiting from all around, but it was also lunchtime and raining heavily, so the shrine was relatively empty. The family got out and searched for Shizuka in the rain, but they found no trace of her. They promptly called the police.

Over 100 police and local firefighters spent 10 days searching for Shizuka's whereabouts but came up with nothing. They combed the mountains near the shrine and sent out sniffer dogs, but again, nothing. Despite the large number of people coming and going for Golden Week, nobody could recall seeing anyone suspicious near the shrine at the time Shizuka disappeared, nor did anyone hear anything suspicious in the rain. It appeared as though she had truly vanished into thin air.

After Shizuka's family returned home, things got even stranger. The family began receiving silent phone calls from numbers in Osaka. The person on the other end never said anything, and they were unable to determine who the calls were coming from as they were different each time. Did the calls have something to do with Shizuka's disappearance? Was it Shizuka herself calling, or perhaps her kidnapper? Nothing ever came of the calls, but it added an extra layer of strangeness to the case.

Seven months after her disappearance, the

television program *Kiseki no Tobira TV no Chikara* aired a special on Shizuka's case. A program that focused on soliciting information from the public about unsolved mysteries, it helped solve 58 of the 138 cases it featured over the years. A home video was sent to the program taken on the day of Shizuka's disappearance. It showed a woman wearing a pink shirt and standing with a red umbrella, but Shizuka's family denied that it was her in the footage. Could there have been two women at the shrine that day wearing the same clothes with the same umbrella at the same time? Unlikely, but not impossible. Further investigation of the video discovered another person standing in the lower right of the screen. Analysis revealed it to be yet another person holding a red umbrella with hair the same length as Shizuka's…

With the case getting nowhere, *Kiseki no Tobira TV no Chikara* then contacted American psychic Gale St. John to ask for her help in finding Shizuka. St. John claimed that a young man approached Shizuka on the outskirts of the shrine asking her for help with something. As they were walking, they came across a middle-aged man lying on the ground. This, supposedly, was what Shizuka's daughter saw her mother doing when she turned around in the car. She was looking at the man on the ground. The young man and Shizuka carried this man back to a car where she was suddenly struck and bundled in herself. She was taken back to their hideout, assaulted, and then the next night driven back to the shrine where she was released. In a daze, Shizuka wondered around the shrine grounds before falling down a cliff to her death.

The psychic's claims produced no leads for police, nor was anything she said ever proven to have actually happened. After all this time, it still begged the question: why? What on earth had happened to Shizuka Noriko?

One theory was that Shizuka ran off, abandoning her family and perhaps running off with another man. This seems unlikely considering that Shizuka stepped out of the car with only 101 yen on her and left her hearing aids, which she needed to function, in the car. If she had been planning on leaving her family behind, why would she go on a trip with them and then leave all of her personal items in the car? It's a possibility, of course, but an unlikely one.

Another theory suggests that Shizuka was involved in an accident. The areas surrounding Akagi Shrine were full of dangerous woodland, and as St. John claimed, she may have fallen down a cliff to her death. This is also unlikely, however, because these dangerous areas were quite a distance from the shrine. The path leading to the main shrine that tourists followed was well maintained and difficult to deviate from. Especially in the heavy rain, it seems unlikely that Shizuka would even want to step off the path, let alone travel so far into the woods that she would fall down a cliff. Moreover, the police combed the woods surrounding the shrine after her disappearance and found no sign of her whatsoever.

A more likely theory is that Shizuka was kidnapped; not by gods, but by humans. Yet this still presents numerous problems. Why was

Shizuka, a 48-year-old grandmother from another prefecture, targeted on this particular day? What was the goal? If it was money, why did the family never receive a ransom request? If it was a random street mugging, why did she disappear without a trace? Why didn't the muggers let her go when they realised she only had 101 yen on her?

It was Golden Week; people were everywhere, and the rain was heavy, so the thieves could have easily escaped into the masses and never have been seen again. It's possible the silent phone calls the family received were from the people who kidnapped her, but why did they never say anything? If they were after money, staying silent about the kidnapping would get them nowhere. Too many details don't fit. No matter how you look at it, there are more questions than answers.

In June 2008, 10 years after her disappearance, Shizuka Noriko was officially declared dead by the courts. No body was ever found, nor any trace of her seen after her daughter last saw her standing in the rain, staring at something across from the shrine. What did Shizuka see that day? How did she manage to disappear from a busy tourist spot during one of the busiest weeks of the Japanese year without a single person seeing her? As outlandish as it sounds in this day and age, it really seemed as though Shizuka had been subjected to *kamikakushi*, disappearing in front of a busy shrine, never to be seen again. No amount of police work, psychic readings, or personal investigations could uncover anything that might have happened to her. It was as though an angry god swooped in and took her away, removing her from this plane of existence.

In August 2012, a human skull was discovered in the forest on Mount Akagi. Hopes were briefly elevated that this might finally solve Shizuka's mysterious disappearance, but the autopsy revealed it to be of a woman in her 20s or 30s. Furthermore, it was likely only a few years old, making it highly unlikely to be Shizuka.

Although she is now legally dead, the fact that Shizuka's family may never know what happened to their beloved wife, daughter, and mother is perhaps the hardest pill to swallow.

Tsujide Noriko Disappearance

Tsujide Noriko was a popular magazine reporter from Ise City in Mie Prefecture. She was hardworking, dedicated to her job, and travelled not only around Japan but all around the world for it. On November 24, 1998, the day after she'd returned from a trip to Thailand—and only two weeks after her 24th birthday—Tsujide stayed late at the office to wrap up some work. She exited the building around 11 p.m. and was never seen again.

What happened to this beloved, hard-working reporter?

The following morning, Tsujide's car was discovered in the parking lot of an insurance company inside the city. It was locked and showed no signs of disarray. It was as though she had parked it, stepped out, and then never returned. Neither her bag nor car keys were inside, indicating that she (or someone else…) had taken them with her. Suspicions grew when police discovered cigarette butts inside the car; Tsujide didn't smoke, and the driver's seat had been pushed back too far for a woman of Tsujide's height to comfortably drive.

Yet despite this, police initially treated the case as a simple "runaway." Tsujide, 24 at the time, lived with her parents—a not all too uncommon arrangement, even with young working women—and despite her parents' protests and fears that their daughter was in danger, the police initially believed that Tsujide had disappeared of her own free will.

It wasn't until December of that same year that

police realised there may have been more to the case than meets the eye, and it was only then that they officially opened an investigation into her disappearance. A person of interest soon rose to the top of the suspect list; a man known only as X who had worked with Tsujide on several articles over the years. They knew each other well enough that they occasionally went out to eat together.

On the day of her disappearance, X had called Tsujide four separate times. When police questioned him, X admitted that he had met with Tsujide after she left her office at 11 p.m. Apparently they had had a misunderstanding about an article Tsujide was working on and he wanted to apologise to her in person. He picked her up from where the police found her parked car, they spoke for a few hours, and then he dropped her off along a highway a short distance away. He claimed that was the last he saw of her. Police didn't believe him, however, and upon further questioning he "admitted" that they had actually had sex before he dropped her off.

Tsujide was in a serious relationship with another man at the time and had never once showed signs of infidelity, nor did she seem the type to cheat, so police grew even more suspicious. They continued investigating X and soon discovered that he had kept a sex worker confined against her will one year prior, so they swept in and arrested him. They hoped more intense questioning would lead to the man admitting his part in Tsujide's disappearance, but on the advice of his lawyer, X clammed up and said nothing.

At his trial for the confinement, X was found not guilty, and as the police were unable to extract any further information about Tsujide from him, they were unable to arrest him on that charge either. In an interesting turn of events, X then sued the police and prefecture for his arrest before dropping the case entirely a few days later without word. He never said anything about why he dropped the case, or why he even started it to begin with.

Although police continued to suspect X in Tsujide's disappearance, investigations were unable to dig up anything connecting him to it and so they stopped pursuing him. With X apparently off the suspect list, the public began turning to other sources to explain her disappearance, and one of the most widely spread rumours claimed that she was kidnapped by North Korea.

In 2008, 10 years after her disappearance, the *Sankei Newspaper* ran an article stating that experts in Chinese and Korean relations claimed "there was a high chance Noriko-san was kidnapped by North Korea." A special committee exists that investigates disappearances such as these to determine whether the victims may have been abducted by North Korean forces, a problem that Japan has been dealing with for several decades. North Korea has admitted to only a few abductions over the years, but Japan claims they may have taken as many as 300 Japanese citizens.

According to the article, investigators spoke with several North Korean defectors who claimed to have seen a woman who looked just like Tsujide in Pyongyang. As a result, the NGO that oversees potential North Korean abductees officially added Tsujide's name to the list. But was she really abducted? Most victims taken by North Korea *were* young women, and they came from all over Japan. It is a possibility, of course, but without proof, we may never know.

One more particularly outlandish theory also grew out of Tsujide's own reporting history. Although she often wrote bright and cheerful lifestyle articles, such as the best restaurants to visit and the best sightseeing locations around town, Tsujide had also been visiting women in Southeast Asia and Thailand and investigating firsthand how they were smuggled into Japan for sex work. As mentioned earlier, she had just returned from a trip to Thailand the day before she disappeared. During her many trips abroad, it was believed Tsujide had discovered many of these women were being smuggled into Watakano Island—an island in Mie Prefecture also popularly known as "Prostitution Island" for its long history of selling women.

As the theory went, the organisation running this trafficking ring discovered that Tsujide was investigating them, so they got to her first. They abducted her the night she went missing and smuggled her to Watakano Island herself, forcing her to work as one of the prostitutes she had spent so long investigating.

Whether you believe this one depends on how deep you like your conspiracy theories to go, but other than Tsujide's investigations into the sex trafficking of women from Southeast Asian countries into Japan, there was no evidence that any of it had to do with Watakano Island, let alone that she was abducted by shady organisations and forced to work there herself.

Watakano is a small island with only 187 inhabitants as of July 2019, and it's located not very far from Ise. Considering the coverage Tsujide's disappearance made nationwide, one would imagine that if she was there, someone would have seen her by now. Yet, there have been more credible sightings of her in North Korea than in Watakano…

The strangeness doesn't end there, either. Three days after Tsujide went missing, her parents received a phone call from a man who claimed to work for Kuroneko Yamato, a popular delivery company in Japan.

"This is Kuroneko Yamata Home Delivery Service. We have a package for OO (Tsujide's younger sister). We'd like to hand this over to her in person, but we don't know where she lives. Please tell us her address."

No matter what angle you look at it from, the phone call was suspicious, and Tsujide's mother thought so as well. Rather than giving up her address, she asked the man on the line to give his number so she could call them back instead. The man gave her a random 12 digit number that didn't exist. However, they soon realised that the final four numbers were exactly the same as the final four numbers of X's phone number. Coincidence? Or perhaps something more?

The strangeness continued when several years after her disappearance, a woman on the television show *TV no Chikara* claimed that she had been visited by Tsujide's spirit.

"I was driving on the expressway in Ise one night when I noticed a young woman with black hair on the hood of my car. Several days later, she appeared in my house. 'Are you, by any chance, Tsujide Noriko?' I asked her and she nodded. Then in a feeble voice she said, '…I'm cold. My body is under water. Please find me.'"

A spirit medium on the same show claimed to see Tsujide's body in a pond; she had apparently been dumped after being murdered. The program searched the pond but came up empty handed. They found no body. Nothing. Tsujide wasn't there.

It has now been more than 20 years since Tsujide disappeared. When questioned by a reporter familiar with her case, Tsujide's parents revealed that they believed their daughter to be dead. Their only wish was for her bones to be returned to them. They keep her car untouched in their garage, and the pain of her loss has never diminished.

Was she killed by a man with a violent past? Or perhaps abducted by North Korea or some other shady organisation and forced into prostitution? Nobody knows, and the scariest part is, perhaps we never will.

Chiba City Married Couple Disappearance

At 6:02 p.m. on May 18, 2001, a 59-year-old company employee by the name of Kinefuchi Kiyoshi clocked out of work. Unbeknownst to him, earlier that day somebody had called his wife's work to inform them that she would be taking a few days off for a "family emergency." Neither were ever seen again.

The case of the missing Chiba couple is a mystery riddled with enigmas. Let's step back a few days earlier to May 15, a Tuesday. It's here that the real mystery first picks up.

Kinefuchi Ikuko, 54-years-old, called her boss Yamada at the job she worked part time. She requested the day off because the police would be coming to visit her that day. Upon later questioning, Yamada revealed what Ikuko had told him over the phone. According to her, the police had informed her that a gang of thieves were working in the neighbourhood. Two had been caught, but one was still on the loose. This man was extremely skilled with computers and possessed a high intellect. The police further informed her that this highly intelligent thief would undoubtedly strike her house soon, and that he was no doubt watching as they spoke. This thief knew not only the layout of her house, but all about her family, their schedules, and other information that only they should know.

At first, Ikuko was suspicious of the man calling himself a police officer, so she called her husband. The officer greeted Kiyoshi cheerfully when he arrived home from work at 7:30 p.m. and informed him of the same information he had shared with his wife before leaving.

The officer was, of course, not a real police officer. Yet despite Ikuko's initial suspicions, the man seemed to have convinced Kiyoshi and the couple's doubts were washed away. At 9 a.m. the following morning, a man who gave the name Hironaka appeared at the couple's house. Claiming to be a forensic investigator, he once again informed Ikuko that the thief on the run was extremely skilled with computers and that he would be able to withdraw money from their accounts without them realising it. The man handed her a damage report sheet and asked Ikuko to fill in the details of their bank accounts so the police could keep a close eye on them for any suspicious activity. She did as requested and confirmed the information with her *inkan* (a personal stamp used as a signature).

A popular scam in the early 2000s, one that continues to this day despite police efforts to educate and eradicate, was the "it's me" scam. Scammers called elderly people pretending to be a child or grandchild, answering with "it's me!" It's a natural human response to say the name of the person you think you're talking to in such a situation, so an elderly person might, for example, hear "it's me!" and respond with "(grandchild's name), is that you?" This gives the scammers a quick in and before the elderly person has time to realise that something's up, they inform them of something terrible that's happened that quickly requires money. Usually it was an accident, unpaid bills, or a fine for something as innocuous as driving without a license.

The key to the scam was not letting the elderly person have the time to realise they weren't speaking to a relative and have them transfer the money as soon as possible. In its heyday, some scammers were swindling elderly folk of close to 700,000 yen a day. It wasn't long until the police caught on, however, and began efforts in warning the public. Once the public were aware, many scammers turned to similar yet different methods of swindling money. On the surface, it would appear that this was what the Kinefuchis were being subjected to.

At 8 a.m. on May 17, Ikuko once again called work and informed them, "The police are coming again today, so I'll be late to work. If they come after 12, then I'd like the day off." She ended up not going in to work. At 10:01 a.m. and 5:41 p.m., Kiyoshi made two separate calls to the real estate requesting that their locks be changed.

The following morning (Friday), the day both of them would last be seen, Kiyoshi left the house at 7 a.m. He clocked in to work at 8:16. Early that morning, a man claiming to be Kiyoshi then called Ikuko's work. He claimed there had been an accident in the family and Ikuko would be taking two or three days off. The person who answered, confused, offered to switch the call over to a supervisor, but the man refused and then hung up. Upon hearing this, Yamada grew worried and decided to visit the couple's house.

He arrived at 10 a.m. Their car was in the garage but nobody answered the door when he rang. Yamada then went to the rear of the house to look inside and found a man standing on the left-hand side. He described the man as 160-170 cm tall, in his early 60s with short hair and an angular chin. Neighbours later saw the same man loitering around the Kinefuchis' house and reported him to the police. Yet when Yamada saw him, the man instantly turned away from him and said, "Don't say anything." Although finding the man suspicious, Yamada assumed the man really was a police officer who was quietly watching the Kinefuchis' house and left him alone.

At 1:45 p.m. that same day, a man wearing a baseball cap and mask visited the bank in front of Chiba Station claiming to be Kinefuchi Kiyoshi. He asked to close his term deposit account and withdrew the 3,500,000 yen still in it. The man was captured on the bank's security cameras and a single still was later released to the public. The man appeared to be in his 50s or 60s, 165 cm tall, square-jawed with broad shoulders, and damaged ears like those who have taken part in martial arts for many years. The logo on his cap appeared to be a mixture of the letters C and D, most likely the logo of the Chunichi Dragons baseball team from Nagoya. It's possible that this man was the same person Yamada saw when he visited the Kinefuchis' house, but it may have also been an accomplice.

At 6:02 p.m., the real Kiyoshi left work, apparently unaware that someone posing as him during the day had called his wife's work to inform them she wouldn't be coming in and then closed his bank account, withdrawing all his money. After leaving work, Kiyoshi disappeared. It wasn't until May 22, four days later, that Kiyoshi's boss grew worried when he hadn't come into work for the last two days.

Like Ikuko's boss, he went to visit their house and found the front door locked, the storm shutters closed, and the garage door open with the car gone. Various letters and leaflets poked out of the packed letterbox. The man called the police right away, followed by the Kinefuchis' eldest son.

Their son arrived at 10 p.m. that same day after leaving Tochigi Prefecture, where he lived at the time. Together with the police, their eldest son entered the Kinefuchis' house. Their son found it highly suspicious that neither of them were home, yet there were no signs that the house had been broken into. He grew even more suspicious when he found his father's suit jacket sitting on top of a chair. His parents were extremely neat and tidy and would never leave clothes lying around. Moreover, there was no sign of his suit pants or business shirt. Their worst suspicions seemed to be confirmed when they found bloodstains in the bathroom that appeared to have been wiped clean.

The police carried out a thorough investigation of the house the following day but couldn't find any fingerprints other than Kiyoshi and Ikuko's. Luminol testing revealed that quite a large amount of blood had been cleaned up from the bathroom and hallway. DNA testing revealed the blood in the bathroom to have been Ikuko's, while that in the hall came from both Ikuko and Kiyoshi. The amount of blood Ikuko lost was "incompatible with life."

By this point it was clear that Ikuko was dead, and highly likely that Kiyoshi was as well. Yet there were no bodies, and their car was gone. Where were they?

Japan has a surveillance network called the N-system. This automated camera system covers all the major expressways around the country, as well as areas of interest such as the heavily trafficked Tokyo and Osaka areas. The cameras record the license plates of all cars that pass by, keeping a record of the time and place of every car in the system. The Kinefuchis' car was seen on National Highway 357 at 2 p.m. on May 19 (the day after they disappeared) going south towards Kisarazu City in Chiba Prefecture. It was then seen again at 4 p.m. in Kinshi, Sumida City, Tokyo. From there, the car made its way towards the Kannetsu Expressway heading towards Nagano. At 7 p.m., the car was seen getting off the Nagano Saku Interchange and then went silent for the night.

The car was then captured on the N-system again the following morning. At 8 a.m., the car was seen on the Nagano Expressway Shiojiri Interchange. Then at 10 a.m. it was seen on the Chuo Expressway Aichi Komaki Higashi Interchange. This was the last sighting of the car until some four months later.

On September 26, the Kinefuchis' car was discovered in Meito Ward, Nagoya. It's important to keep in mind that the man seen impersonating Kiyoshi at the bank was wearing a Chunichi Dragons baseball cap, the team for Nagoya, making it highly likely that he was a local. The car had been left parked in a no-parking area. The police attempted to lift fingerprints from inside the car but it had been wiped clean. However, they did discover urine on the backseat and the blood of both Kiyoshi and Ikuko in the trunk…

A picture was being painted, but there were still large portions of it missing. Piecing together what the police had learnt, the most likely scenario was that the man or men posing as police officers were in fact intending to scam the Kinefuchis of their money. Whether the scammers intended to kill them from the beginning was unknown, but that Friday night when Kiyoshi returned home from work, Ikuko was killed and Kiyoshi attacked as well. It was unknown whether Kiyoshi died in the house or later in the car, but both bodies were put into the boot, their house cleaned of blood, and then the murderer/s drove their car from Chiba to Nagoya over the weekend. Presumably the bodies were dumped somewhere along the way, and then their car abandoned at the destination. It wouldn't be discovered until four months later.

Yet further investigations revealed even more puzzling questions.

On May 16 at 7:37 a.m., the day after the first "police officer" showed up and two days before her disappearance, Ikuko sent an email to one of her colleagues:

Subject: How are you? I'm not good.

Contents: There's been an incident. It's up there as one of the three biggest, most troubling incidents of my life. So much so that I'm debating whether I should go in to work today. I was depressed the whole day yesterday. I wonder if I'll be able to work after this? I'm relying on OO (name blurred). Thank you. From Ikuko.

Unfortunately, Ikuko's colleague didn't notice this email until nearly a week later on May 22, several days after her disappearance. By the time Ikuko sent this email on Wednesday morning, all she had done was speak to the fake police officer with her husband. That "officer" had informed them of a prowler on the loose that was targeting their house. That was all. How could this simple conversation have ranked as one of the three worst incidents of Ikuko's life? The puzzle pieces didn't fit. Unless, of course, Ikuko wasn't telling the truth…

The information about the police officers visiting Ikuko's house on May 15 and 16 came from Yamada, her boss at work. She was the one who informed him of the conversation that took place, that some police officers were on the lookout for a skilled thief who was targeting her house. The only people aware of what really took place were Ikuko and her husband, and as the police continued their investigations, things took yet another unexpected turn.

Police received Ikuko's broken PC from her eldest son and they were able to restore hundreds of sent emails. Over 100 of them were related to a pyramid scheme selling makeup. Rumours had spread around the workplace that Ikuko had borrowed a rather large sum of money related to the scheme, potentially up to one million yen. When she was unable to pay that back, the person who lent her the money sent yakuza around to get it. It wasn't uncommon for yakuza to pose as police officers to extort money from people at the time (and, it should be noted, the yakuza were especially large proponents of the "it's me" scam once it got into full swing).

Suddenly a different picture was being painted. The rumours were, of course, rumours. No-one could confirm or deny whether Ikuko was in any debt, nor whether the fake police officers were yakuza members. Yet it seemed more likely, especially with the discovery of Ikuko's involvement in the pyramid scheme, that she was in some type of financial trouble.

The fake police officers were not there to warn her about a thief that was, for some unknown reason, specifically targeting her house, but were actually debt collectors. Rough-looking gang members suddenly showing up on the doorstep of an elderly couple would quickly raise alarms in their small neighbourhood, but people wouldn't think twice about police officers. Ikuko being in debt large enough to send collectors to her home would certainly rank as one of the three most troubling incidents of her life, as opposed to an unknown thief targeting her house.

The yakuza have a large presence in Nagoya,

with the Kodo-kai, one of the largest syndicates in Japan, based there. The man captured on bank security cameras withdrawing Kiyoshi's money wore a cap of the local Nagoyan baseball team. After the couple disappeared, their car was discovered abandoned in Nagoya. Was this unassuming elderly couple truly killed by the yakuza because of an unsettled debt? The truth is, we may never know.

Nearly 20 years have passed since the couple disappeared, and the main suspect, if still alive, would be in his 80s by now. There are still numerous missing pieces to the puzzle and details that don't make sense upon closer examination. Was it truly a yakuza hit, or perhaps something else entirely…?

Sakaide Takenoko Digging Girl's Disappearance

Goshikidai Visitor's Centre sits only a few short kilometres from the Seto Inland Sea in Kagawa Prefecture. Sitting atop one of the numerous peaks in the Goshikidai area, the centre educates visitors about the surrounding national park, as well as holding numerous events and activities for all to enjoy. One of these activities is a bamboo shoot digging event. These edible shoots, known in Japanese as *takenoko*, are extremely popular in many Japanese dishes and are harvested in the spring and summertime. On April 29, 2005, however, something was about to go terribly wrong.

On the morning of April 29 (Friday, a public holiday), the Goshikidai Visitor's Centre held a flower viewing event. Onishi Yuki, 5-years-old, attended with her mother (42) and older sister (8). She was seen in another participant's home video asking questions about the flowers and wearing a pink hat, striped orange and white long-sleeved shirt, purple pants with orange stripes running down the sides, and pink shoes. All colours that would make her easy to spot amongst the trees.

Then in the afternoon, a bamboo shoot digging event was held. 19 families (54 people) gathered for the event with six volunteers for a total of 60 participants. The Onishi family were amongst them. The event began at 1 p.m. with a scheduled end of 2 p.m. Participants would then gather in a gazebo outside the bamboo forest.

At 1:30 p.m., Yuki and her mother stepped off

the path to dig up another shoot. It was Yuki's fourth of the day and she was getting more and more excited. As her mother dug it up, Yuki told her, "I'll go find another!" She ran back towards the path, and that was the last her mother ever saw of her.

When she hadn't returned by 2 p.m., Yuki's mother grew worried and began looking for her. She went to the designated gazebo but when she wasn't there either, the rest of the participants learnt the girl was missing and set out to look for her. With no sign of the girl by 3 p.m., the Goshikidai Visitor's Centre alerted police. Police arrived 45 minutes later to begin searching, and at 5 p.m. the fire department also showed up. Police dogs were deployed and over 100 people searched until 9 p.m. that night. There was no sign of her.

For the next few days, upwards of 200 people continued to search the bamboo forest, as well as the woods to the north and the nearby pond, but to no avail. The pond was eventually drained but neither the little girl nor any of her personal items were found in it. So, what happened to her? How could a five-year-old girl vanish at an event with more than 50 other people around?

In 2008, three years later, a television program ran a special on Yuki's disappearance. According to them, two people had seen the little girl after she left her mother's side; one of them a junior high school student, and another an adult man. The junior high student revealed that she had passed Yuki walking along the path and they exchanged a few words before continuing their separate ways.

The man said that at 1:40 p.m., 10 minutes after Yuki had left her mother to find more shoots, he saw the girl walking zig-zag along the path to the south of the gazebo. If both of these accounts were true, that meant that Yuki followed the path clockwise after leaving her mother.

Yuki disappeared on a Friday. This particular day happened to be the first day of the Golden Week holidays. While not consecutive, by taking one or two days of private leave in between, many workers would have been able to get 10 days off in a row. This allows people to travel all around the country, and places like Goshikidai are popular locations to get away from it all. The area features camp grounds, various forests and hiking trails, as well as numerous other scenic sights that bring people from all around the country to take in its beauty. Had one of those people also taken Yuki?

Numerous tourists from the camping grounds were interviewed at the time of Yuki's disappearance, but none had seen her. If the early eyewitness testimony was to be believed, Yuki was moving away from the campgrounds anyway, not towards them. Was it possible that someone, possibly a tourist, had kidnapped Yuki from the event area away from nearly 60 pairs of eyes? Had they bundled her into a car and taken off, swiftly returning from whence they came? Or was it, perhaps, a local who knew the area well enough to abscond with a small girl so that no-one would see them in the act?

The actions and strange movements of the police dogs sent to find Yuki caused even more concern.

The first dog was given Yuki's water bottle to sniff. It soon picked up her trail and followed it through the bamboo forest before stopping at a small hole in the ground. The dog wouldn't go any further. The following day, another four sniffer dogs were sent out to follow Yuki's trail. They followed it to the same spot as the first and stopped before the same hole, not moving any further.

The September 16, 2005 episode of *Super Friday* aired a special on Yuki's disappearance and they addressed the strange nature of the dogs' actions. A specialist claimed that the only reason Yuki's scent would have disappeared on that spot was if she was somehow lifted into the air, for example, by a helicopter. Even if another person, like a kidnapper, picked her up from that spot and ran off with her, the dogs should have been able to follow her scent regardless. Their trail would transfer from the little girl's feet scraping along the ground to that of the person carrying her. The fact that the dogs stopped and that spot and wouldn't go any further was truly puzzling. The program then set up an experiment to test his theory.

For the experiment, a small girl was to walk from Point A to Point B. This would mimic Yuki's known movements. Then, a man would pick the girl up and walk from Point B to Point C. The dogs would follow the girl's trail, and if they continued from Point A to Point B, then Point B to Point C—with the girl being held in the air by a man and thus not touching the ground—that would prove the specialist's point that she couldn't have been carried away, otherwise the dogs would have picked up the trail.

The dogs were given an item of the girl's to smell and set out. They followed the girl's trail from Point A to Point B, as it was expected they would. The problem was the next step: Point B to Point C. Would the dogs stop at Point B, where the man picked the girl up and carried her through the air, or would they be able to follow her trail all the way to Point C? If they stopped at Point B, then it would suggest that it was possible a man abducted Yuki from the forest and carried her away. If they continued to Point C, then it would suggest it was highly unlikely she was carried away from that spot, otherwise the five dogs sent out to find her would have continued on.

The dogs, upon reaching Point B, continued without hesitation to Point C. It appeared the specialist's theory was right, and based on the experiment alone, it was unlikely that Yuki was picked up from before the hole and carried off. So, if she wasn't carried off, what happened to her? Why did the dogs all stop at the same point in the middle of the forest?

This is one of the more mysterious points of Yuki's disappearance. Nobody knows why the dogs all stopped on the same spot. It's been suggested that the dogs lost the trail because so many people were passing through. 60 people were taking part in the bamboo shoot digging event, and then many more police and firefighters over that same night and following day. It was possible that Yuki's scent disappeared because it was masked by so many others. It certainly made more sense than Yuki being abducted into the sky.

Others also criticised the experiment for its poor design. It didn't replicate the actual conditions of Yuki's disappearance. For the experiment, a girl walked from Point A to Point B, a man picked her up and carried her from Point B to Point C, and then the dogs were sent out to follow the trail. If they were to accurately replicate the conditions of Yuki's disappearance, then they should have sent groups of people out to walk back and forth over the same spot, and leave at least several hours between the man carrying the girl away and releasing the dogs.

Numerous theories have been proposed over the years as to what really happened. Perhaps she fell into Tanbe Pond, situated just to the right of where the participants were digging. The man who saw Yuki for the last time spotted her not too far from the pond, and the dogs also stopped just a few metres to the left of it. However, as it was mentioned earlier, the pond was drained and no signs of the girl found, nor did anyone find any skid marks on the banks (which sloped gently towards the water), nor did anyone hear any screams or splashes.

Another theory, and perhaps not an awful one, is that Yuki got lost in the forest. The bamboo forest was just a small section of a much larger mountainous forest region. It's not hard to imagine the little girl wandering off the path to look for bamboo shoots and not realising that she'd gone too far.

This theory was bolstered by the fact that the police dogs only searched the area north of the bamboo forest; they never sent the dogs to the east, west, or south. It's unknown why they didn't, but perhaps they felt the girl wouldn't have gone that way; to the south lay the visitor centre, to the east Tanbe Pond, and to the west a road and car park leading to the visitor centre. It's also unknown how far north the police searched; perhaps they didn't go far enough, thinking that the girl couldn't possibly have gone that far. The chances of this are still low, especially taking the sniffer dogs into consideration, but it's a possibility. However, if Yuki really had walked north and gotten lost all by herself, it stands to reason that the dogs would have picked up her trail somewhere.

As with many of these mysterious cases, some theories were more outlandish than others. Some claimed she was eaten by a bear, she was eaten by a monkey, she was attacked by a crocodile, a bird of prey carried her off, a childless couple kidnapped her; the list goes on. There was one more theory that held a little more weight, however; the theory that Yuki was kidnapped by a paedophile.

According to eyewitnesses, a man was seen near the bamboo shoot digging event on the day Yuki disappeared with a large ruck sack on his back. This alone wouldn't be terribly suspicious; it was a national park with numerous forests and mountains to climb, so a hiker carrying a ruck sack would hardly be a rare sight. But this man was seen disappearing into the forest, heading towards the bamboo area. Witnesses found this strange because the man wasn't on any of the paths, and closer investigation revealed he had followed a much smaller animal trail, suggesting he knew the area well and knew how to get in and out of places away from the public eye.

If the man were a local, it was possible that not only did he know the Goshikidai area well, but he knew of the bamboo shoot digging event as well. 60 participants in a densely wooded area, many of them with children. Children who would be likely to step away from their parents for short bursts at a time to go looking for bamboo. For a person well versed in the area, all it would take was waiting for the right opportunity to pass by. Like little Yuki as she stepped away from her mother.

As mentioned earlier, it was also the beginning of Golden Week. Tourists from all around the country would be mixing with locals as they enjoyed all the park had to offer. This does raise the suspicion that more eyes would thus make the crime more difficult to carry out, but that's not necessarily true. If we assume for a moment that Yuki really was kidnapped by a local with a large ruck sack, more eyes wouldn't have to mean trouble. How many tourists are really going to take notice of another man walking through the forest with a large bag on his back? He's just another tourist, like them. Better to blend in and slip by than try to sneak around and look suspicious.

This potential kidnapper may have known of the bamboo shoot digging event, planned his crime, waited for the opportunity to grab a child and then knocked her out, stuffing her in the bag and casually leaving the area. The sniffer dogs all stopped at the same spot, and despite the experiment performed on

TV to test whether the girl was carried off or not, the number of people trampling over the area in the meantime could easily have masked her scent. This seems far more likely than an unseen helicopter or UFO lifting her into the air. Once the man got her back to his car, he could have disappeared anywhere and her body never seen again.

In 2015, 10 years after Yuki's disappearance, Fuji TV aired a special called *Saikyo FBI Kinkyu Sousa SP*. The show brought in former FBI investigators from the US to see if their expertise could shine new light on the disappearance. The team brought in cadaver dogs from the US to search the area, but they found nothing. If any trace of Yuki remained, even a decade later, the dogs should have been able to find something, but they couldn't. While not 100% proof, once again it seemed likely that Yuki had been kidnapped and taken from the area. Yuki's parents participated in the search for their long-lost daughter once more, and the man with the ruck sack was again brought up, but nobody had any new information on who he might have been.

What really happened to Yuki on that fateful day? Kidnapping seems the most logical choice, but there are still numerous unanswered questions. 15 years have passed since she was last seen; if Yuki were still alive today, she would be 20-years-old. Is she still out there somewhere, perhaps unaware of her past, or did the unthinkable happen, and Yuki is no longer with us? For Yuki's parents, no doubt they spend every day wondering what happened to their little girl and whether she'll ever come back, but the signs, unfortunately, do not look good.

Balloon Man Incident

In the 2009 film *Up*, the elderly widower Carl ties thousands of balloons to his house so he can set out and see the wilds of South America, thereby fulfilling a promise he made to his late wife in the process. For Japanese audiences, this no doubt brought back memories of a somewhat similar incident that really did take place in Japan during the 1990s.

Suzuki Yoshikazu was born in 1940. His family ran a piano tuning business and, after graduating from the National College of Music in Tokyo, he started work at Yamaha as a piano tuner himself. He was also a self-styled adventurer. In 1984, he opened his own business selling teaching materials for music, and then in 1986, he opened his own music salon. He then opened his own mahjong and coffee stores, as well as a pub restaurant. Yet despite, or perhaps because of all these businesses, by 1990 he was 500 million yen in debt. He told his creditors that he planned to pay them back, but when he told them how, they were astounded; he planned to sail across the Pacific Ocean in a gondola held up by balloons.

Suzuki never explained exactly how he planned to make 500 million yen from sailing across the ocean in a gondola held up by balloons, but he immediately set about making it happen.

On April 17, 1992, Suzuki set out on his first test flight. Now 52-years-old, people had taken to calling him the "Balloon Guy." For his first trip, he planned to travel from the Tama River in Fuchu,

Tokyo, to Kujukuri Beach in Chiba Prefecture. He tied four giant balloons full of helium—two five metres wide and two three metres wide—to a special chair and strapped himself in. The police, of course, attempted to stop Suzuki, but he shook them off and took to the air.

News cameras and media followed Suzuki as he sailed, keeping a close eye on him. Within 30 minutes he'd reached a height of over 4000 metres, the wind slowly moving him through the air. The temperature at that height lowered to -11 degrees Celsius, causing the media to fear for his safety, but he showed no signs of distress.

Everything was going to plan and his flight appeared to be going quite well until 1:20 p.m., when one of the ropes holding his weights snapped. This caused the balloons to sail higher than intended, sending him flying 5,600 metres above the ground. Suzuki responded by cutting one of the larger balloons off with his lighter to equalise the weight. Although this succeeded in keeping him from going any higher, the loss of helium was too much and he quickly began descending into the city. Suzuki crashed landed on a private rooftop in Ota Ward, 24 kilometres from where he had taken off. He walked it off with only a sprained wrist. The test flight was, by all accounts, a success.

The police strongly reprimanded Suzuki, but he had no plans of stopping. He announced his next flight would be all the way to Hawaii, astounding onlookers. Then on November 23 of the same year, Suzuki prepared for his next trip, this time in a gondola he nicknamed *Fantasy Gou*. A master basket maker from Edogawa in Tokyo reportedly built the gondola especially for him. It was made of Japanese cypress, a highly buoyant material in case of an emergency. The gondola measured two metres wide and long, and one metre high. Attached to it were six vinyl balloons with a diameter of six metres, and 20 smaller balloons with a diameter of three metres; a considerable upgrade from his first flight.

Inside the gondola he prepared a week's worth of food, various flying instruments and maps, arctic clothing, and weights made of Japanese *shochu* (liquor) that he planned to drop as the flight went on to lighten the weight. He figured that the gas would gradually deplete over the course of his trip, so to maintain height, he could drop the weights at regular intervals.

The flight of November 23 was held under the pretext of being a test flight, and he was joined by university professor Miwa Shigeo, seven of Miwa's students, an *Asahi Newspaper* reporter, and crew from the television program *Ohayou! Nice Day*. They gathered on the shores of Lake Biwa in Shiga Prefecture, and the plan was to raise the gondola to 200 or 300 metres and then safely bring it down again. They rose the gondola to 120 metres before returning safely to the ground, but then at 4:20 p.m., Suzuki threw off the gondola's moorings and called out, "I'll be back!"

"Where are you going?" Professor Miwa called out, to which Suzuki answered, "America!" He dropped some bottles of shochu in the gondola to level out his height and set out for his goal of Sand

Mountain in Nevada. According to Suzuki's hard-laid plans, if he could reach a height of 10,000 metres, he could ride along the jet stream and reach America in 40 hours.

It doesn't take a genius to figure out that flying from Tokyo to Nevada with nothing but a few helium balloons wasn't likely to work, but Suzuki was determined to make a point. Or, depending on who you spoke to, was just plain crazy. Perhaps his massive debt had pushed him over the edge; his years of business failures finally caused him to snap, and he figured he had nothing left to lose. Either way, Suzuki was in the air held aloft only by balloons, and all people could do was watch.

The Japanese Coast Guard and media kept a close eye on Suzuki once more, and at 6 a.m. the morning after he set off, Suzuki called his family from his cell phone. "The sunrise is beautiful!" he said. "I'm going to go as far as I can, so don't worry!" That was the last his family ever heard from him.

The following day, November 25, Suzuki sent out an SOS call. The Japanese Coast Guard found him at 8:35 a.m. roughly 800 metres to the east of Kinkasan in Miyagi Prefecture. He had travelled half the length of Japan in two days. Yet when Suzuki saw the search and rescue aircraft, he waved and signalled that he was okay. They continued to monitor the gondola held aloft with balloons, which sat at a height of 2,500 metres—although at one point it reached as high as 4,000 metres in the air—for three hours before it disappeared into the clouds. The coast guard lost sight of him and was forced to pull back. That was the last anyone saw of him.

On December 2, Suzuki's family officially filed a missing person's report, and the Japanese Coast Guard contacted Canada, the United States of America, and Russia with details of the case. No countries reported either Suzuki or the *Fantasy Gou* washing up on their shores.

So, what happened to the infamous Balloon Guy? The most likely scenario is that he crashed somewhere in the Pacific Ocean, and with how massive it is, neither his body nor the gondola were ever found. Some have speculated that he may have fled to another country to escape his debt, or perhaps even found his way back to Japan where he started fresh with a new identity. Others claimed that Suzuki knew the trip would kill him and it was a planned suicide. If still alive today, Suzuki would be in his 80s, but considering how famous he was at the time, if Suzuki really had survived and found his way back to Japan, chances are good that someone, somewhere, would have recognised him.

Suzuki left behind a wife, Yukiko, whom he married only six months before his trip (his third marriage). She reportedly never gave up waiting for his return, and all three of her daughters from a previous marriage went on to graduate from music school, a passion they shared with their stepfather. One of his stepdaughters, Fumiko, went on to debut as a musical artist and also worked as an actress in the NHK drama *Hikeshi ya Komachi*. In 2000, Yukiko herself released a book called *Fuusen Ojisan no Chouritsu* (The Balloon Guy's Tuning). In it, she spoke of the events leading up to Suzuki's flight and disappearance, and also of her dreams, thoughts, and memories of her missing husband. She reportedly never gave up hope of his return, and refused to move from their house because if she did, then he might not be able to find his way home to them. Yukiko passed away in 2017 from liver cancer, only a year after she finally remarried a man from Portugal.

Before she passed away, both Yukiko and the remaining members of Suzuki's family were said to be paying off his debt. Whether they've finished paying it off yet is unclear, but just because he disappeared, it didn't mean his debt did as well. Perhaps something to keep in mind for future adventurers hoping to outrun their money problems.

Chiba Junior High Student Kidnapping

"Hey, what are you doing out here so late at night? It's illegal for children under 16 to be outside without their parents after 11. You over there, come with me."

On October 26, 1991, Sakuma Nana and three of her friends were having a get together. The young teenagers were first graders at a junior high school in Chiba Prefecture and had just finished their midterm exams. It was a Saturday night, and they had no school or club activities the next day, so to celebrate, they gathered at Sakuma's house for a sleepover.

Sakuma (13) was a single child who lived in an apartment with her mother. Her mother worked in a snack bar, so she was at work while the girls ate, drank, and talked at home alone. Shortly after midnight the girls ran out of food, so they decided to go to the convenience store to restock.

The majority of convenience stores nowadays are open 24 hours a day, but in the early 90s this wasn't the norm. The girls rode to a nearby store but it was already closed, so they had to ride to the nearest 24 hour store in Oguradai, over four kilometres away. A typhoon had just passed through Chiba Prefecture a few days earlier, so the roads were covered in debris. Junior high school students use their bikes to get everywhere, regardless of the weather (even today), so a four-kilometre ride after midnight didn't faze the girls in the slightest. They got on their bikes and rode down National Highway

126 towards the convenience store.

The girls arrived 30 minutes later. They stocked up on tea, chips, pizza, and onigiri, then got back on their bikes to return home. On the way, however, Sakuma ran into a tree lying across their path and fell from her bike. She was okay, but her three friends got off their bikes to join her and for a short while the girls remained on the spot, perhaps giving Sakuma a chance to recover from her fall.

Before long, a man walked by, stopped, turned around, then called out, "Hey, what are you doing out here so late at night?" The man, short, stout, and in his 50s, told the girls he was a "protective counsellor" (no such role existed in the area) and that "it's illegal for children under 16 to be outside without their parents after 11." The girls, only 12- and 13-years-old, naturally panicked. They had been making quite a bit of noise on the sidewalk after midnight and genuinely believed they were in trouble.

The man continued. "I should let the police know about this, but just today I'll let you off if you tell me why you're out. You over there, come with me." The man pointed to Sakuma and told the other three to go home. The girls, afraid and panicking, asked the man what they should do with Sakuma's bike. "I'll take it back later with my truck," he said, and so the girls, frightened and confused, left. It was the last time they would ever see their friend.

The three girls returned to Sakuma's house, but Sakuma had the key, so they were unable to get in. They waited outside for an hour and a half for her to return when two boys from their class happened to pass by. The girls ran down to tell them about what happened, and the boys immediately knew that something was wrong. Only then did the girls finally call their parents and let them know what had happened.

Sakuma had been kidnapped.

Her mother was informed and the parents first searched the nearby area themselves, but were unable to find any trace of the girl. At 4:20 a.m. on October 27, they went to the Chiba Higashi police station to file a missing person's report.

According to the girls' descriptions, the man who took Sakuma was 155 centimetres tall, of stocky build and in his 50s. He had thin, almond-shaped eyes, and was wearing a striped long-sleeved shirt with black pants and a black knitted cap. He kept his hands in his pockets as he spoke and squared his shoulders in an attempt to intimidate the girls.

Sakuma, only 13 at the time, stood 150 centimetres tall and weighed 42 kilograms; she was a tiny girl and described by many who knew her as beautiful. It has long been suspected that this was the reason the man singled her out of the group. Neighbours who saw her riding on a unicycle in front of her apartment when she was younger claimed she was so cute that "we thought she could be an idol."

Investigations turned up several key sightings of Sakuma and her kidnapper after the girls left, piecing together a brief, if incomplete timeline of their movements immediately thereafter. Between 1:20 and 1:30 a.m., a driver saw a young girl and older man matching Sakuma and the kidnapper's descriptions at an intersection in Sakazukicho, a short distance from where the man first approached the girls. The pair were again seen at 2:15 a.m. near the Chishirodaikita Monorail Station. They appeared to be on foot and heading northwest.

The final sighting of the pair was at 4 a.m. in a residential area of Chishirodai. After that, the pair disappeared, and neither of them has been seen since. Security cameras weren't commonplace at the time, so it was impossible to track their movements on the streets other than the few eyewitness reports the police were able to dig up. All the police could determine was that the pair continued on foot for several hours in a north-westerly direction after the man told Sakuma's friends to leave, and they were last seen in a residential area several kilometres north of Sakuma's home.

Then she was gone.

One theory that soon emerged was that, like many others, Sakuma had been kidnapped by North Korea. The area Sakuma was taken from was said to be a known route for North Korean spies to kidnap Japanese people before smuggling them out of the country. Some claimed that the particular language the man used (claiming to be a "protective counsellor"), in addition to his threatening manner and attitude which allowed him to kidnap a girl right out of her friends' hands, could only be the work of a professional.

Yet others disputed this; it was too random. The man only came across the girls because Sakuma hit a tree lying across her path and then the girls decided to spend some time there. Plus, if the man really was a North Korean spy, it would have been more likely for him to kidnap all four girls, rather than show his face to all but only take one. It's not impossible that the man was a North Korean spy, but it's a lot of coincidences to add up while ignoring other key factors.

The most common theory is that the man was simply passing by and saw an opportunity. Judging by his movements afterwards, the man knew the area well. He may have been waiting to kidnap a girl, patrolling the streets night after night, or he might have just happened upon Sakuma and her friends while out and seized the moment. Either way, there was no way for the man to know the girls would be passing by at that moment, but it's not difficult to believe that the man may have been passing by, heard the girls making noise, and then stopped to observe them before making his decision. Sakuma was a beautiful girl, and she in particular was singled out from her friends. Plus, if the kidnapping had been planned from the get-go, why didn't the man have a truck ready? Why did they walk across town for two hours before disappearing?

What the man was doing out so late at night has long been a subject of debate, as well as where he took Sakuma in the early hours of that Sunday morning. Did the man take her home? To a hideout? To an accomplice's house? Did they get on public transport and go somewhere else? What was he doing in that area and why did they walk so far?

Why didn't the man have a vehicle nearby?

Many have wondered why Sakuma didn't call for help when the man forced her to walk for several hours across town, but it's important to remember that Sakuma was only 13. She was in the first grade of junior high and said to be a quiet, introspective girl. The man, while not physically large, was still bigger than her and rather imposing. He may have threatened the girl's life once they were out of earshot of her friends, so it's possible the girl was too afraid and confused to do anything.

It's also been suggested that perhaps the man was a thief who was canvassing the nearby factories and homes. This would explain why he was out so late at night and the type of clothes he was wearing. He may also have been a truck driver, as some have surmised his comment of "I'll take it (Sakuma's bike) back later with my truck" was delivered too quickly and smoothly to have been made up on the spot. That would also explain why the man didn't care if the girls saw his face. He may have been out walking late to keep himself awake, and in either situation, just happened to come across the girls. And their long walk across town? He may have been taking her back to where his truck was parked. He may have known the area from previous visits, but didn't live in town and thus didn't fear anyone seeing his face.

A montage photo was created of the main suspect and police also created posters with a likeness sketch of the man they were looking for. The case, however, quickly went cold. Several decades later, a man by the name of Naka Katsumi was arrested for killing a high school girl in Kyoto and abandoning her body in a copse of trees. The man shared an uncanny resemblance to the suspect last seen with Sakuma in Chiba, and the internet went into an uproar thinking they had finally solved the case. There was a problem, however; Naka—who received the death penalty in 2014—was 67-years-old at the time of his death. This meant he would have been in his early 40s at the time Sakuma was kidnapped; the suspect was said to be in his 50s, so somewhat older. Maybe the girls got his age wrong? It's possible the man looked older than he really was, after all. But that wasn't the only problem; Naka had been arrested on a different charge a month before Sakuma's disappearance. He was in jail at the time, and so couldn't have been involved.

In the years following her disappearance, Sakuma's mother was often seeing praying in front of a statue of a frog at a nearby temple for her safe return. The words *buji kaeru* were carved beneath it, which is a common play on words. *Kaeru* means frog, but it also means to return. *Buji kaeru* literally means "safety frog," but it also means to return safely. Statues of frogs are often inscribed with these words to pray for someone's safe return.

Sakuma's mother ended up moving back to her parent's house after her daughter's disappearance, but she continued to rent the apartment in case her daughter ever returned. Neighbours never saw the lights on after that, but she left a window open for her daughter to get inside, just in case. It wasn't until 2005, 14 years later, that she finally vacated the apartment for good.

The statute of limitations on Sakuma's disappearance has long since passed, and if still alive today, she would be in her early 40s. Her kidnapper would be in his 80s. Sakuma's mother has reportedly never given up hope of her daughter coming home one day, but with each day that passes, it seems more and more unlikely. And as for what happened to her after she was last spotted several kilometres north of her house in Chiba, again, we may never know.

ROBBERIES

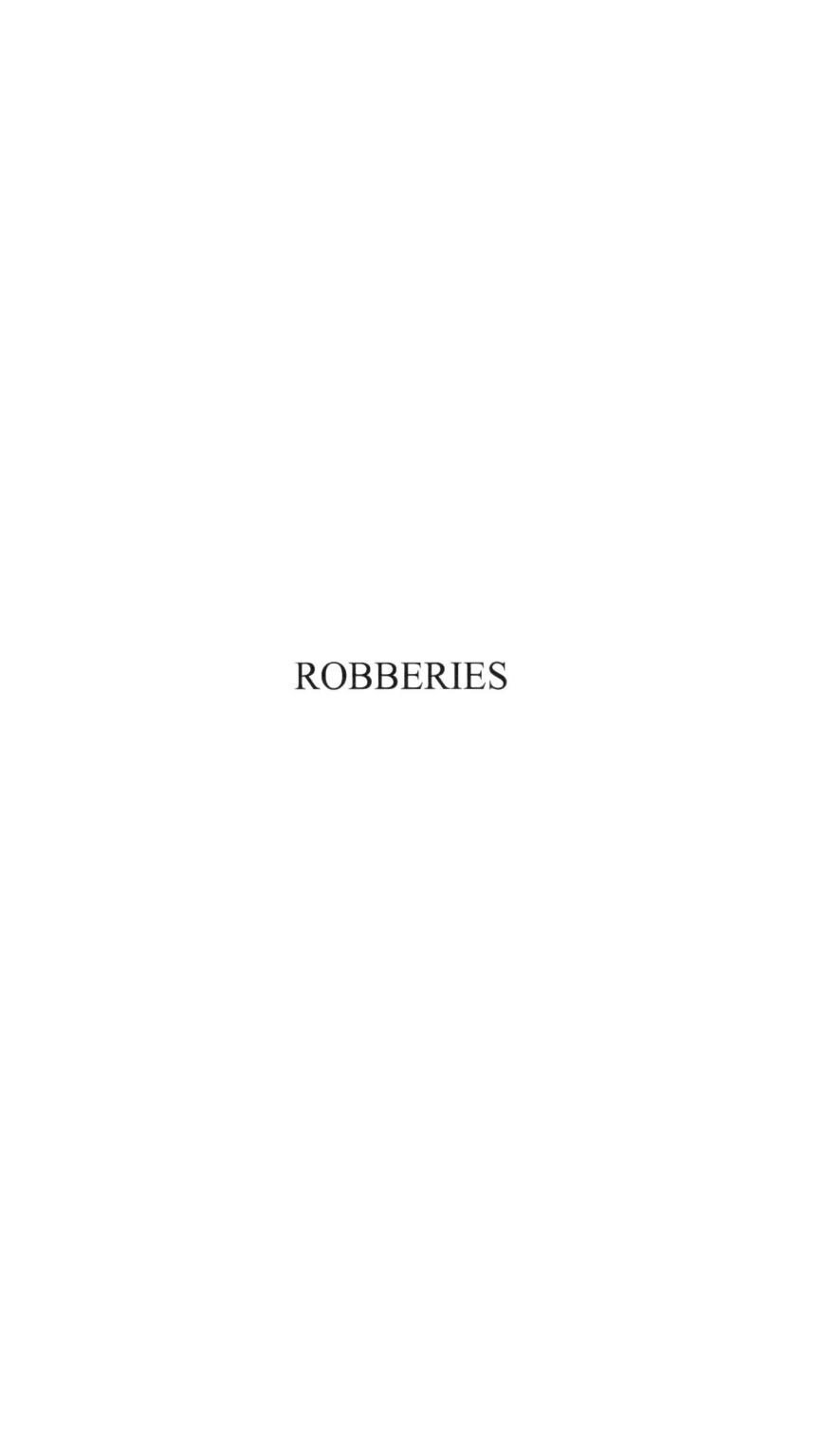

300 Million Yen Robbery

The late 1960s saw Japan still recovering from its World War II loss. The country was in the process of rebuilding, both structurally and economically, and it was a time of heavy student movements. Numerous protests were held against the Treaty of Mutual Cooperation and Security between the United States and Japan, as many students didn't like the terms set out in it, and the country itself was in a constant process of upheaval. Amongst this volatile environment, the single largest heist in Japanese history was carried out. It came to be known as the 300 Million Yen Robbery, and it remains unsolved to this day.

At 9:20 a.m. on December 10, 1968, four employees of the Nippon Trust Bank were transporting 294,307,500 yen worth of bonuses for the bank's employees. Bonuses are paid out to full-time employees usually once or twice a year (summer and/or winter), depending on the company, and this can amount to a hefty sum of money. The cash for these bonuses—nearly 300 million yen—was kept in three metal boxes inside a security car.

At 9:30 a.m., as the transport vehicle approached Fuchu Prison, it was pulled over by a man in uniform on a white police bike. He chased them down and then pulled out in front of the car, forcing them to stop. The driver wound down his window to ask what was wrong, and the officer explained that their branch manager's house had exploded. He also claimed they had received news that dynamite had been attached to the car they were currently in, so he would like to investigate it. The branch manager of the Kokubunji Branch had indeed received a threatening letter four days earlier. It demanded the manager send a female bank clerk with 300 million yen to a designated location the following day or they would blow up his house. 50 police officers staked out the scene at the time designated in the letter, but the perpetrator never showed up.

With this knowledge in hand, the bank employees believed the officer and let him investigate the car. He crawled under it and, before long, the men saw smoke billowing out. "It's going to explode! Run, quickly!" the officer screamed. The bank employees abandoned the vehicle and, as they did, the officer jumped into the driver's seat and took off, leaving his bike behind.

At first the men thought the officer was trying to get the car away from the impending explosion, and even praised his bravery, but when the "dynamite" on the ground fizzled out, they soon realised something was wrong. The "dynamite" was nothing more than a flare the man had lit to get them out of the car. After it extinguished without exploding, the men realised they had been duped, and 300 million yen had been stolen from right beneath their noses. Closer inspection of the white police bike also revealed it to be a fake; it was a stolen bike that had been painted white. The men called the police.

At 9:50 a.m., 10,000 officers were deployed all over the Tokyo Metropolitan area to find the car. It was discovered abandoned, the boxes with the money empty roughly 1.5 kilometres away. The thief had abandoned the car and driven off in another stolen vehicle, before changing into yet another stolen vehicle after that. It's believed the thief switched vehicles at least eight times during his getaway; six cars and two bikes were thought to have been stolen and prepared beforehand. At the time, such vehicle swapping while on the run wasn't especially common, and the police struggled to track him. In the end, they were unable to find him, and he got away with 300 million yen in cash.

The bank employees all received their bonuses without problem the following day; the money was paid out by insurance, which in turn was paid out by other insurance, all the way up the line before finally ending with an overseas insurance company. Ultimately, it was this overseas insurance firm that footed the bill for the stolen money, leading some to call the case the "incident where nobody in Japan suffered damages."

The thief left behind over 120 pieces of evidence, many of them designed to throw the police off his trail. While these included the vehicles he used to escape in, he also deliberately dropped stolen everyday items to confuse investigations. These included things like everyday trash (cookie tins, magnets, newspapers), clothing (hats, raincoats, female earrings), and other random items (magnets, a megaphone, gambling items) he had gathered from all around the country.

Police found saliva on the stamp used to send the threatening letter to the branch manager. It was discovered to have come from a person with type B blood. The note itself was sent using letters cut out from a magazine, so they were unable to investigate the handwriting, but they discovered that a page from the same magazine was wrapped around the flare used to confuse the men at the scene of the crime, leading police to believe it was the same person involved in both.

The same style of writing and the particular words used in the threatening letter (lingo unique to workers in the telephone industry) also closely matched a case that had taken place earlier that year. Known as the Tama Agricultural Cooperative Threatening Incident, the Tama Agricultural Cooperative in Tokyo received threatening letters and phone calls lasting from April 25 to August 22. They were threatened with arson and bombs if they didn't hand over money, much like the Nippon Trust Bank branch manager. The letters also made reference to the Yokosuka Line train explosion that took place on June 16 that same year. Whether the same person was also involved in that was unknown, but on November 9—a month before the 300 million yen robbery—a 25-year-old man was arrested for the explosion. He was executed on December 5, 1975, right before the statute of limitations on the bank robbery expired. Considering he was in police custody when it took place, it seems unlikely he was involved.

Because no violence was involved in the robbery, the statute of limitations on the crime was only seven years, meaning it passed on December 10, 1975. The statute for a civil liberties case expired 20 years later on December 10, 1988. But that's not to say that the police didn't exhaust all options in the meantime in trying to catch the criminal.

Montage photos were released shortly after the crime based on descriptions from the bank employees, and the man was said to be in his early 20s. 114,368 people were questioned during investigations and 25,357 pieces of evidence taken into account. On top of that, 171,805 investigators worked the case at some point, making it one of the biggest in Japanese history. Nearly 200,000 police officers worked on the case, and yet this young man still escaped with not even a hint as to who he may have been.

One clue, which ultimately went nowhere but for a short while tantalised police, was discovered on the megaphone the man used when posing as a police officer. The megaphone, like the bike, had been painted. Investigators discovered a piece of newspaper beneath the paint only 2 millimetres wide, but it was enough to let them know that the perpetrator had likely painted the megaphone at home, and to keep the paint from getting everywhere, he used newspaper to keep things clean. If they could discover which newspaper the scrap came from, they would be able to tell the general area the criminal was from.

Meticulous detective work revealed the 2 millimetre scrap came from the *Sankei Shimbun* December 6 edition, four days before the incident. They matched one of the characters in the scrap to a heading from the paper, and then traced the distribution route to the areas west of Tokyo, including parts of Kanagawa and Saitama

Prefectures. However, by the time they had determined this, two years had already passed. The subscriber information the newspaper kept which recorded the names of customers and where they lived for that time period had already been destroyed. If they had been a little quicker in uncovering the information, they may have had the criminal within their reach.

Numerous people were interviewed as suspects over the years, ranging from gang leaders, real estate agents, company employees, and even electricians; all people who somehow, in some way, could have been involved in the crime, but ultimately were proven innocent or there wasn't enough evidence to convict them. Investigators believed the crime to be the work of a single person, judging by his actions before and after the theft.

One main suspect that people still talk about, however, was the son of a policeman. 19-years-old at the time of the crime, he had a history of stealing cars, was good with motorcycles, and he knew all sorts of information about police procedures thanks to his father's job. The young man committed suicide five days after the robbery, however, and investigations of his house turned up nothing. Police investigated every little piece of information they could about the man's movements around the time of the crime but were unable to find anything linking him to it, and according to reports, he had spent the night before the crime drinking in Shinjuku. This wouldn't have given him the necessary time to prepare all the escape vehicles he needed beforehand.

The public were enthralled by the idea of a policeman's son carrying off the biggest heist in Japanese history, however, and dramatisations of the crime in novels and television programs have often taken this route when explaining it. Over 20 novels have been written about the crime over the years, in addition to 13 television dramas, seven movies, five comics, and one theatre play. Then, in August 2018, a writer posted a story on the website *Shousetsuka ni Narou* (Let's Become Novelists) claiming to be the actual perpetrator of the crime 50 years after the fact.

The writer posted their story to the site, which allows regular updating of stories chapter by chapter that anyone can read, and then collected everything for a proper book release in December of the same year. News of the "real" perpetrator finally stepping out of the shadows and laying claim to their handiwork brought the crime back into the forefront of the public's consciousness, but at the same time, many people doubted its authenticity.

The statute of limitations on the crime had long passed. The criminal could absolutely come forward with undeniable proof that they had stolen the 300 million yen and nothing could be done about it. But by the same token, that also meant that anyone else could come forward claiming that they had done it and have their five minutes of fame as well. Details of the crime were well known. All it would take was filling in some blanks with a little imagination and an audience willing to believe; an audience who already wanted answers to one of the greatest mysteries and biggest crimes in modern Japanese history.

The reception to this person claiming to be the real criminal wasn't all good, however. Many complained that the story read more like a bad romance novel with some details of the crime mixed in. Others accused the language of being unlike what a 70- to 80-year-old would use (the age the criminal would be today if still alive). Aspects of the story were criticised for being too "modern" and lacking in authenticity of the time the crime took place.

The person, calling himself Shirota, claimed to have led a happy, peaceful life, now surrounded by children and grandchildren. The reason he was revealing all was because his wife had recently died in an accident, and on the advice of his son, he was now ready to reveal all. Shirota claimed to be the friend of the policeman's son who committed suicide five days after the robbery. It was Shirota, struggling academically, who went to his friend Shogo (the policeman's son) with plans to steal the money.

Shogo was in a relationship with a girl by the name of Kyoko, who Shirota also liked. The love triangle obviously complicated matters and in the end, the pair ditched Shogo and planned to take the money themselves, allegedly leaving Shogo's father's police notebook by the empty money cases as they escaped.

It was this detail of the police notebook that led many to wonder if "Shirota" really was the criminal, as it wasn't a piece of information known by the public. Yet the other suspicious aspects of the story couldn't be disregarded, and as of this book's publication, Shirota's novel currently holds a 2 1/2 star rating on Amazon out of 5, with 39% of the ratings being 1 star. One reviewer even noted that at the end of the book, in tiny letters, it states, "This novel is a work of fiction." Yet another 21% are 5 star ratings, proving that even now the book is still highly divisive, and many enjoyed the story even if it was fake.

We may never know the truth. Even if the real thief is still alive and they come forward, there's no way for anyone to know for certain that they're telling the truth. Perhaps if they had some vital detail about the crimes that only the perpetrator would know it might be easier to believe, but those who would know those details—the original investigators—would also be in their 80s and 90s if still alive today. No doubt the investigators most of all would love to know who carried out the biggest heist in Japanese history—and got away with it—but only time will tell whether someone steps forward with irrefutable evidence, and with each day that passes, that time frame gets shorter and shorter.

In the end, we may never know, but that's part of what makes it so fascinating, isn't it?

MURDERS

Shimane Female University Student Corpse Discovery

On October 26, 2009, Hiraoka Miyako, a first-year student from the University of Shimane, left the shopping centre she worked part time at after work. A native of Kagawa Prefecture, 19-year-old Hiraoka entered the University of Shimane in Hamada City, Shimane Prefecture, with the intention of earning her degree and then working overseas to help developing countries. She was a hard worker, both at school and work, and participated in her university's volunteer club. She was, by all accounts, a model student and dedicated to her future goals. That night after she left work, she was never seen again.

Hiraoka's parents filed a missing person's report with the police two days later. On November 2, the Shimane police officially opened their investigation into her disappearance, a full week after she was last seen. Hiraoka was not the type of student to skip class or even show up late, nor was anybody aware of troubles she may have been having. Her disappearance was suspicious, and both her friends and family worried for her safety.

On November 6, four days later, a woman's severed head was discovered near the summit of Mount Garyu, a mountain close to the border of Shimane and Hiroshima prefectures, roughly 25 kilometres south of Hamada City. It was Hiraoka's. The very next day, the Shimane and Hiroshima police departments announced they would be working together to find the perpetrator of the horrific crime. The whereabouts of the rest of Hiraoka's body remained unknown at the time.

The day after the press conference, part of Hiraoka's left thigh bone was discovered. The flesh had been cleanly cut off and not a drop of blood remained. The day after that, her limbless torso was found wrapped in a vinyl bag. Perhaps in an attempt to disguise her identity, Hiraoka's body had been mutilated. Her breasts had been cut off, displaying her rib cage below, and the internal organs of her lower body had been removed. There was also evidence that the perpetrator had tried to burn her. The following day her left foot was discovered, and then on November 19, her nails. The rest of her body was never found.

The horrific nature of the crime led police to believe that someone had a grudge against Hiraoka. They investigated suspicious vehicles that had been in the area the night she went missing, her associates, and even went so far as to make a list of people who had rented splatter films from the nearby video store. Yet they got nowhere, and no suspects stood out.

It was determined that Hiraoka was killed sometime between her disappearance on October 26 and October 31. Judging by the state of her remains, she had been dumped on the mountain soon after death. Her head showed signs of blunt force trauma and a high possibility of strangulation, while her body had been cut up with a small, sharp knife. Police profiling suggested that the killer was cruel, destructive, stubborn, and eccentric. The killer was likely to be a man in his 20s to 40s, worked alone, was familiar with the area, and dumped the body in the early hours of the morning due to the high amount of traffic Mount Garyu received during the day. The only evidence they had to work with was the vinyl bag they found Hiraoka's torso in. It was a polyethylene bag used by NTT to distribute phone books. The bags varied by year and area, and this particular bag was used in five different cities near Mount Garyu during 1995, 14 years before the murder took place.

On December 26, two months after Hiraoka's murder, the police opened a toll-free number for any information related to her death. The case had already hit a standstill, and the police were no closer to catching the perpetrator. Another two months later, on February 26, 2010, the police announced a reward for anyone with information leading to the killer. A further two months after that, on April 26, the police distributed leaflets appealing to the public for information about the case. All leads had dried up, and the police were no closer to solving the brutal murder. Who could have done it, and why? All the police had to go on were the remains of the woman's body. They had no motive, no suspect, and no other clues.

This lack of progress on the case continued for several years, and on October 26, 2012, the statute of limitations for abandonment of Hiraoka's corpse expired. The police announced their intentions to continue investigating the case as a murder, but no new information had been uncovered in the years that had passed. The police once again distributed leaflets regarding the case, but they seemed to have hit a dead end. Nobody had any clue who the killer might have been. Was it somebody close to Hiraoka? A random attacker? Was the murderer still out there killing others, or was it a onetime attack? Why was Hiraoka murdered in the first place, and so brutally at that?

By 2016, seven years after her death, more than 310,000 people had been involved in the investigation into Hiraoka's murder. In December of that same year, police began looking into people who lived near the area with a history of sex crimes. There, one particular suspect stood out; Yano Yoshiharu, a businessman for a solar panel company who lived in the nearby city of Masuda at the time.

Yano was born in Shimonoseki, a city to the south of Yamaguchi Prefecture. He grew up there with his parents and younger brother and was captain of the track team in junior high. He was a shy student who had trouble talking to girls, and this didn't change when he entered high school. Although he was handsome, with people often saying he took after his mother's good looks, he struggled with the opposite sex and threw himself into study instead, with classmates calling him serious and diligent. During this time he also earned his black belt in judo.

Although he was initially accepted into the National Defence Academy of Japan with flying colours, Yano chose to go to a regular national university in Kyushu instead. Here, in contrast to his younger days, Yano opened up and spent all his time chasing after women. It consumed his mind so much that he ended up dropping out of school altogether due to his lack of desire to keep studying. He took part-time jobs and even formed a band with one of his friends. The band did well, and he threw his all into it, but after an argument with his close friend and band mate, things ended badly and they broke up.

Then in 2004, Yano was arrested. He had attacked and sexually assaulted three women from various parts of Japan. He picked the women randomly from the street, threatening them with a knife before assaulting them. He spent three and a half years in jail for the crimes, and roughly two years after release, started working for a solar panel company based in his hometown of Shimonoseki. Yano was a salesman and good at his job, bringing in high sales to the company, but he also complained a lot and showed signs of stress. Nobody knew of his past, and he was working in Hamada City at the time Hiraoka was attacked.

To the police, suddenly everything fell into place. Here was a man with a history of violent sexual crimes, and he was in the area at the time of the attack. Finally, a real suspect. But there was one big problem; Yano was dead. In fact, he had died only two days after Hiraoka's severed head was discovered on Mount Garyu.

After seven years, the Shimane and Hiroshima police finally seemed on track to cracking one of their most brutal and baffling cases in recent memory... but their prime suspect was dead. He died in a car accident with his mother on a Yamaguchi highway two days after Hiraoka's head was discovered, and one day after news of her murder had been made public. But it didn't end there.

The police went to visit Yano's family home in Yamaguchi Prefecture numerous times. His younger brother continued to live there with his wife, and neighbours reported seeing the police seize many of the suspect's personal items which had yet to be thrown away. Amongst these items the police found a digital camera and USB stick. The contents had been deleted, but they were able to recover the files. They revealed 57 photos showing Hiraoka's brutal murder; the knife thought to have cut her head off, bruising around her neck that indicated strangulation, and photos of before and after her head had been severed. The photos were taken in Yano's rental house in Masuda, clearly showing his bathroom in the background. Over a period of an hour and a half, Yano meticulously documented his dissection of the body through photos. The police had finally found their man... but he was already dead.

Piecing together events, Hiraoka was likely abducted on her way home from work by Yano, who was also working in the area that night. He took her back to his home in Masuda, a 45-minute drive away, and strangled her to death. He then dissected the body and drove the pieces to Mount Garyu where he dumped them. Yano continued going to work afterwards as though nothing had happened.

Hiraoka's severed head was then discovered on November 6, and an announcement made to the public on November 7. On November 8, Yano then told friends that he would be visiting his father's grave with his mother (his father having died two years earlier). Their car crashed on the way home and both occupants died. The police had spent seven years looking for a man who had died in an accident only two days after his victim was discovered. The two cases were, unsurprisingly, never connected. It was also around this time that the police discovered the vinyl bag Hiraoka's body had been found in was also distributed in one more place outside Hiroshima; Shimonoseki, Yano's hometown.

Even though the suspect was already dead, police filed documents with the Matsue Public Prosecutor's Office. They claimed to have enough evidence that would easily put Yano behind bars if he was still alive, but on January 31, 2017, the Prosecutor's Office announced that, due to the suspect's death, the case was being dropped. Just like that, the long investigation into Hiraoka's bizarre murder was over. The killer had been dead all along in a random and unrelated car accident that nobody knew about.

Nagaokakyo Bracken Gathering Murders

Two housewives, referred to in the media as Housewife A and Housewife B, finished their part-time jobs at the local Izumiya supermarket shortly before lunch on May 23, 1979. Both women worked as shelf packers on the 6 to 10 a.m. shift. A, 43-years-old at the time, and B, 31-years-old, then each bought a *bento* lunch box from the store and left together. They got on their bikes and made their way towards a nearby mountain to pick some bracken. The mountain, referred to by locals as Noyama, was famous for both bamboo shoots and bracken, both of which locals collected for home cooking. The plan was to collect some bracken, eat lunch together, and then return home. B had to pick her child up from kindergarten at 3 p.m. that day, so she couldn't be out too late.

The women parked their bikes by the field in front of the Jakushoin temple at the foot of the mountain around 11 a.m. Construction was taking place nearby and the guard on duty saw the women, as well as several other villagers nearby at the time. It was A's seventh time that year gathering bracken from the mountain, but it was B's first. It was also the last time either of them was seen alive.

What happened next is unknown. It's assumed the women climbed the mountain, ate the lunch they'd bought from the supermarket, and then started gathering bracken. When neither of them returned home that night, B's husband grew worried. He went to search the mountain alone, worried when his wife hadn't picked up their child from school, but he couldn't find any trace of her. A's husband, working the night shift, didn't notice his wife was missing until he returned from work the next morning. At 2:50 p.m. on May 24, the following day, the men submitted a missing person's report with the Muko City police.

A search party 30 strong was organised and set out to find the women. They soon found the women's bikes by the Jakushoin temple, and the guard from the nearby construction area revealed he'd seen the women enter the mountain trail around 11 a.m. the previous day. The search continued late into the night, but they found no trace of them.

The search continued at 9 a.m. the following day. This time a team of 120 people, including the police, fire department, and the women's family and friends set out with three sniffer dogs to comb the mountain. As they reached the mountain peak close to 10:30 a.m., one of the sniffer dogs reacted. A's body was found lying on a steep slope off the side of an animal trail, face up and head towards the bottom of the mountain. Roughly 10 metres away they found B's body, lying face down on the slope.

A was dressed in jeans and a sports shirt. The buttons of her shirt had ripped off and were lying on the ground nearby. She was also missing her shoes, but her jeans were still on. There were strangulation marks around her neck, and she was covered in more than 30 bruises, likely from being punched and/or kicked. Nine of her ribs had been broken and her liver ruptured. In addition, the investigators discovered semen inside her body, which when tested later proved to come from someone with type O blood. It was immediately clear that she had suffered a horrific assault that had led to her death. Her bag was found nearby with her wallet and money still in it, along with the bracken she'd gathered and her empty bento box. The reason for the attack did not appear to be a random robbery.

Likewise, B was also discovered with strangulation marks around her neck, and over 50 different bruises from her assault. Unlike A, however, B was discovered face down in the grass, her bag still on her back. Her lower half was naked, with her panty hose and underwear bunched by her feet. Her underwear had been torn, and her jeans and shoes were discovered on the ground nearby. She had clearly put up a fight.

When they turned B's body over, they discovered a large kitchen knife sticking out of her chest. Her shirt had been rolled up, and the knife thrust directly into her skin. The autopsy revealed blood loss from this wound was what ultimately killed her. The knife had broken her fourth rib, piercing her heart all the way through to her lungs. Although B's jeans and underwear had been removed, the investigators were unable to find any semen in her body. Her vaginal walls were torn, however, suggesting the perpetrator had violated her with a foreign object before death. And although the officers couldn't find any semen, they did discover a hair that came back as blood type O, same as the semen discovered in A's body.

Something awful had clearly happened to these

two housewives while they were gathering bracken. Investigators discovered a bundle roughly 10 cm wide of the plant in their bags, so they had been at it for a while, and both their lunch boxes were empty. Their stomach contents were examined during the autopsy and the state of digestion suggested the women had been killed roughly an hour after eating, so probably around 1 to 2 p.m. B had to pick her child up at 3 p.m. that day, so they were likely getting ready to leave when they were attacked. Even stranger, however, was a note the police found in A's jean's pocket:

We're being chased, please help us, this man is evil.

The note was written in pencil on the back of a receipt from Izumiya. The receipt was dated two days earlier. The police were unable to find a pencil nearby and ended up sifting through the top layer of soil near where the women's bodies were discovered. They found a piece of lead one centimetre long roughly 17 metres south of B's body, but no sign of a pencil. The writing was a strange mix of all three Japanese writing systems, but handwriting analysis confirmed that it was most likely written by A, perhaps as they were hiding or on the run from their attacker due to its sloppiness. The note suggested they were attacked by a single man, and DNA from a person with type O blood was discovered on both of them, lending more credence to the theory.

So, who did it? Who committed this horrific crime, brutally murdering two women and abandoning their bodies on the mountainside? The police had little to work with. It was likely a single man with type O blood, although the possibility that two or more people had been involved couldn't be ruled out. Other than the semen and the hair, they had nothing to go off. They were unable to find any fingerprints, even on the knife.

The police initially tried to trace the sale of the knife found in B's chest, hoping this would lead them to the attacker. The knife was stainless steel with a brown wooden handle, 30 centimetres in length with an 18 centimetre blade. It was one of 70,000 knives made in Gifu Prefecture, but that particular production line had ended several years earlier. It came without a maker's seal, meaning it was sold through an outlet store as extra stock and thus impossible to trace. The knife was a dead end.

Investigations pulled up several suspects, however. One was a middle-aged man in his 40s who had been seen in the area the previous year. The man, roughly 170 centimetres tall and wearing grey clothing, approached a woman who was gathering bracken about 300 metres to the southwest of where the housewives would be murdered. Holding a 30-centimetre-long knife, he asked the woman, "Ma'am, can we gather bracken here?" Seeing the knife, the woman panicked and fled to where her husband and child were collecting bracken nearby. The man was never seen again.

Another suspect, who may or may not have been the same man, was also seen in the area shortly before the murders. This man was also described as being in his early 40s, and judging by his appearance, a businessman. He had been seen three times, only ever on Wednesdays or Thursdays. He had been seen approaching women and asking if it was possible to gather bracken in the area, just like the man with the knife had the year before. The housewives were, perhaps not coincidentally, murdered on a Wednesday... A likeness of the man was drawn up, but the police never discovered who he was.

This man, or men, weren't the only suspects, however. Police also questioned two delinquents who were known gang members in the area. Different sources gave them different ages, but they were said to be around 28-years-old, with one potentially younger than the other. Both men were seen fleeing from the mountain around 2 p.m. on the day of the crime. One of the men was experienced in karate, and they often got into violent fights. Both men were seen whispering about something in front of their house the night of the crime, placing them high on the police's suspect list. However, the men turned out to have an alibi, with the boss from the construction company they worked at vouching that they had been at work that day.

Investigations revealed that, despite being a weekday, 15 to 16 people were on the mountain gathering bracken and bamboo shoots that day. Construction was taking place at the foot of the mountain, with numerous people coming and going and several vans and passenger cars parked nearby. Was the perpetrator a local? Someone passing through? The few leads the police had went nowhere, and no arrests were ever made. But that wasn't the end of the strangeness.

On May 15, 1984, almost five years to the day later, another housewife was killed in Nagaokakyo. Referred to as Housewife C, this woman was stabbed to death in the neck and back, wrapped in a futon, and then set alight. It didn't take long for people to try to connect this case to the other housewife murders five years earlier. Rumours quickly spread that it hadn't been two women gathering bracken on the mountain that day, but three. C, the third housewife, had joined the other two later (or was perhaps already on the mountain when they arrived), but when the attack happened, she was able to flee and get away.

Why C would remain quiet and not go to the police if this was true is unknown; but rumours being rumours, people claimed that she was there, and her escape only delayed her death. Some suggested that C *had* gone to the police, but they kept her involvement in the horrific attack quiet for her own safety, and the media then agreed to go along with it. Public knowledge of a survivor would put her and her family at risk after all, alerting the attacker to her identity.

It's hard to deny the eerie similarities. Like A and B, C had been strangled and assaulted, and like A and B, DNA evidence revealed her attacker to have type O blood. But was it truly the same man? The police never once alluded to any connections between the cases, and nobody in the media ever came forward with any evidence of a cover up. This part of the rumours is nowadays considered to be an urban legend, but just like A and B's murders, C's murder was never solved either.

The statute of limitations for the murders of A and B passed on May 24, 1994. Nobody ever confessed to the crime, and if it really was the man in his early 40s that the police suspected, he would be well into his 80s by now. At this point, it's unlikely we'll ever know what really happened on that horrific day, and whether the murder of another housewife five years later was in any way related.

Wednesday Strangler Incidents

Over a period of 14 years in the 1970s and 80s, seven women from Saga Prefecture were kidnapped, strangled, and killed. Of these seven, only one disappearance did *not* take place on a Wednesday, leading to the incidents being collectively known as the Wednesday Strangler Incidents. More formally, it went by the name the Saga Seven Women's Serial Murders. Of the seven women, five were confirmed to be strangled, while the other two were nothing more than skeletons by the time they were found.

The first victim to go missing was Yamazaki Tomiko, a 12-year-old girl in the first grade of junior high who lived in Kitagata City (now Takeo City). On August 27, 1975 (Wednesday), her mother left for work at 4 p.m. Reports on what exactly her mother did at the time were conflicting, but she worked in the food industry. Several years later she ran a snack bar, so it's highly likely— especially taking her working hours into account— that she also worked in a snack bar at the time. Either way, Yamazaki's mother left for work in nearby Shiroishi City at 4 p.m., leaving her daughter home alone. Yamazaki occasionally joined her mother at work and studied in the waiting room, but on this particular day she stayed behind.

Yamazaki's friend came over to her house for a few hours before leaving around 7 p.m. Yet when her mother arrived home from work around midnight, Yamazaki was nowhere to be seen. The lights and TV had been left on, and her futon pulled out to sleep. Her shoes were untouched and there was no sign of a struggle. It was as though she had vanished into thin air. Her mother searched the neighbourhood for her, but when she couldn't find her, she filed a missing person's report with the Omachi police on August 28, the following day. The police were unable to find any leads, however, and the case quickly went cold. Sometime over the next few years, Yamazaki's mother moved away from Kitagata City to Saga City, roughly 30 kilometres away.

The next woman to go missing was five years later. Hyakutake Ritsuko, who was 19 at the time, worked part time at a cafe in Omachi. She lived with her parents, older sister, younger brother, and younger sister. Those around her considered Hyakutake a serious young woman. After junior high, she left Omachi to go to nursing school in Hyogo Prefecture, and after graduating there, returned to Saga and went to another nursing school close to home. In 1978, she started working part time at the cafe Linden; the owner's daughter was a classmate of her older sister. Her time at the cafe and various nursing schools had made her many friends, both male and female, but around the time of her disappearance it was believed that she was having troubles with the opposite sex. In particular, she had been seen making calls to a male acquaintance from the cafe.

Hyakutake was a hard worker who never missed work, but before her disappearance, she had attempted suicide twice over her troubles. Rumours soon spread that she had proclaimed she wished to commit suicide on her upcoming 20th birthday, and she had scrawled in a notebook at work *"All I can think about is* him.*"* "Him" was apparently Hyakutake's older sister's boyfriend. Supposedly he was seeing both of them, and two weeks before she disappeared, Hyakutake left behind evidence that she was about to go on a trip. When her friends spoke to her about what to give a friend for her upcoming wedding, she reportedly answered, "I have no time for such matters, I have more serious things to think about."

At 11:30 p.m. on April 12, 1980 (Friday), half an hour before her 20th birthday, Hyakutake disappeared from her house wearing her favourite negligee. At the time, her father was hospitalised with an injury so her mother was by his side. Her sisters were also spending the night elsewhere, and her brother was working in a different prefecture. She was all alone. Just like Yamazaki, Hyakutake's shoes were found in the house and there was no sign of a struggle.

Her parents, aware of the rumours that she wished to kill herself on her 20th birthday, quickly set out to find her. However, three days after her disappearance, her father received a letter written in old fashioned script. It consisted of three lines. The first line was never released due to information pertaining to the family's privacy. The second and third lines, however, went as follows:

Your daughter's not coming back.
Suffer.

They also received phone calls telling them not to go on TV or release their daughter's photo.

Two months after her disappearance on June 24, a sanitation worker was cleaning the toilet tanks at Suko Elementary School in Omachi (this cleaning took place once every two months) when he opened the lid and discovered a body inside. It was Hyakutake. She was naked, floating face up and covered in stones to weigh her down. Her face was decomposed beyond recognition, but the police were able to grab a fingerprint from her left thumb to verify her identity. The police from Shiroishi and Omachi joined forces to investigate her murder and squads were sent out to comb the areas surrounding the school for evidence.

As this was taking place, the vice principal made another request of the police. Reportedly, the school requested cleaning for a separate set of toilets on June 18 because the school pool was about to open for swimming season, but the tank was full of rocks so they couldn't get in. When the police investigated, they found yet another body.

It was Yamazaki.

Two young women had gone missing from the same area in the space of five years. Yamazaki (12) in 1975, and Hyakutake (19) in 1980. The women had no apparent connection to each other, and yet their bodies were found in separate toilet tanks on the same school grounds, both covered in rocks. Five years had passed since Yamazaki had gone missing, so her body was little more than bones with some hair. She was still dressed in the clothes she wore the day she went missing, and the police quickly contacted her mother, now living in Saga. When she saw the clothes, she broke down into tears and nodded over and over, confirming that it was her daughter. The reason no-one had discovered her body over the five years since her disappearance was because people rarely used those toilets. The path leading to them was rough and full of snakes, so when pool season came around, children used different toilets instead.

An autopsy was performed on Hyakutake's body the day after she was discovered. It was determined that she died one to two months earlier by suffocation. Nothing foreign was discovered in her lungs, meaning she was likely killed elsewhere and then dumped in the tank after. Further investigation of the tank revealed her pantyhose and a syringe, as well as a single slipper and a child's sandal (which were considered unrelated to the case). According to the sanitation company, the last cleaning had taken place on April 21, more than a week after her disappearance. They noticed nothing strange with the tank at the time.

On June 10 (two weeks before Hyakutake's discovery), the students of Suko Elementary School were cleaning near the toilets when a girl found a clump of red hair. She threw it away, but the police later found and tested it. It was Hyakutake's. Hairs were also discovered on the tank lid, suggesting the body had been in a state of decay when it was put in. The date her body was dumped was narrowed down to between April 21 and June 10, with her death taking place sometime during April 12 and April 21.

Considering the similarities in their disappearances and deaths, it seemed likely that Yamazaki and Hyakutake had been killed by the same person, and as it turned out, the police *did* have a suspect in mind.

On March 12, 1981, 29-year-old U (name never officially released) was arrested by the police on a separate charge of attacking a factory worker. He was, however, also a prime suspect in Yamazaki and Hyakutake's murders. And who exactly was U? U was the man dating Hyakutake's older sister. The man she was thought to be cheating with. Rumours said that U wanted to marry her older sister, but her parents were against it, making him resentful. In addition, he was also said to have connections to Yamazaki, being a regular visitor to her mother's bar. Even after her mother moved to Saga City and opened another bar, he reportedly went to visit her there several times.

The police arrested several of U's friends and tried to extract information from them, but they were unsuccessful. What they did know was that he was a violent man with close connections to both victims, and he also lived in Shiroishi, close to the school both bodies were discovered in (U was a former student of Suko Elementary, so he knew the area well).

He had no alibi for the time Hyakutake went missing, and during police questioning revealed that he had been drinking in Shiroishi the night she disappeared until 11 p.m., but after that he went home.

Investigations of his home discovered stationery

that matched the threatening letter sent to Hyakutake's parents, and a handwriting analysis confirmed there was a high probability that it was his as well. The police arrested U for a second time, but still he denied taking part in her murder. In the end, the police had nothing substantial to connect U to the threatening letter or Hyakutake's murder (having the same stationery wasn't a crime) and handwriting analysis wasn't enough to convict in court, so he was released.

Things took another turn for the strange when sometime later, a woman anonymously called the police.

"I'm from Omachi, but I got married and live in Takeo City now. I was returning home (to Omachi) for some business one night when I happened to see a man carrying a woman into a car next door. My relationship with my mother-in-law isn't very good, so if I tell you my name, combined with the fact that I've briefly returned home, she'll find out and get upset. As such, I can't tell you who I am."

Investigations quickly identified the woman as the daughter-in-law of the family who lived behind Hyakutake's house and called her in for questioning. However, the woman had no memory of ever making such a call. The police refused to believe that it wasn't her and ended up doing voice print matching to confirm the truth. When the first test didn't come back with the results they wanted, they performed a further two tests before finally believing her.

So then, if it wasn't her, who called them? It was clearly someone who was close to the woman, as they knew the details of her present circumstances. Why would they remain anonymous? Why would they pretend to be someone else? The police were at a loss, and ultimately, never found out who it was or why.

A year and a half later, a third victim appeared. On October 7, 1981 (Wednesday), 27-year-old Ikegami Chizuko went missing. A married woman from Shiroishi who worked for the sewing company Rimusu, she went grocery shopping around 5 p.m. after work. She was last seen in the supermarket car park talking to a man in his 30s in a reddish-brown car. One of her colleagues saw her and remarked that they seemed to be friendly.

It should be noted that Ikegami had been missing from work for the previous four days without word. When she returned, she informed her workplace that she had been caring for her ill mother. However, suspicions were raised when she then went missing, and both her family and workplace filed missing person's reports with the police.

Ikegami's body was discovered two weeks later on October 21 in Nakabaru (now Miyaki), roughly 40 kilometres away. She was found in a fenced-off abandoned lot and, judging by the state of decomposition, had been dead for one to two weeks. She was identified by the Risumu uniform she was still wearing. There were no signs of sexual assault and her cause of death was determined to be strangulation. An electrical cord had been wrapped around her neck four times, leaving massive bruising. Police had no suspects.

A fourth victim appeared six months later, this

time an 11-year-old girl from Miyaki, the same city where Ikegami's body was discovered. At 4:20 p.m. on February 17, 1982 (Wednesday), fifth grader Nishiyama Kumi left school with two of her friends. They parted ways roughly 250 metres from the school and that was the last anyone saw of her. When Nishiyama didn't arrive home, her worried parents alerted the police at 8:40 p.m. that night.

A search party was organised the following morning and her body then discovered in a field halfway between her school and home. She was lying face down, her school bag on her back and her lower body naked. She had been sexually assaulted and then strangled to death with her own stockings. This field was less than two kilometres from where Ikegami's body had been discovered six months earlier.

Unlike Ikegami's case, this time the police did have a suspect. Although Ikegami had last been seen talking to a man in a reddish-brown car, a man in a white car was seen loitering around Miyaki before the attack. Thought to be in his 30s or 40s and described as having a high-bridged nose and sharp, thin eyes, he was seen earlier that day trying to pick up a housewife near the then Kewpie Market Mae bus stop. He asked her, "Want a ride?" but was so persistent when she refused that she threated to call the police, finally forcing him to leave.

At 2 p.m. the same day, the same white car was seen outside Mitagawa Elementary School, roughly five kilometres from the Kewpie Market Mae bus stop. He called out to a young girl from his car, telling her, "I have some Pink Lady (a famous pop duo) photos to show you, so come over here." He then grabbed the girl and carried her into the girl's toilets, but when she screamed, he ran off.

At 3:10 p.m., he then approached two girls walking home from Kitashigeyasu Junior High School before moving on to three elementary second graders 20 minutes later. He told the girls he would drive them home, but they refused. An hour later, Nishiyama would go missing.

At 4:30 p.m., a housewife saw the man's white car parked on the side of the road, close to where Nishiyama's body was found. Considering the time Nishiyama was last seen and the location of her body, it was likely the man was with her at the time. The car had a Fukuoka number plate.

Considering the location and method of both deaths, the police were looking into the suspect for both Nishiyama and Ikegami's murders. A likeness of the man was published three days later in the February 20 edition of the *Saga Shimbun* newspaper.

This particular case then took a turn for the strange when one of Nishiyama's close friends received a call on February 18—the day after she went missing—at 7:15 in the morning. When the girl's mother answered the phone, a female voice said, "This is Nishiyama, is OO-chan there?" The mother informed the caller she'd already left for school and they hung up. Nishiyama's dead body was found four hours later. Nobody ever discovered who made the call, but it was somewhat reminiscent of the mysterious call police received years earlier regarding Hyakutake's disappearance.

The following day, a letter addressed to "Miyaki City, School, Health Care Centre" stated *"I intended to hold the girl ransom, but she wouldn't stop making a fuss so I killed her."* Another strange phone call and another strange letter, just like in Hyakutake's case.

At this point, it was unclear whether these first four murders were related. At the very least, Yamazaki and Hyakutake's murders seemed connected to the same suspect, and Nishiyama and Ikegami's murders potentially shared the same suspect, although this connection was less clear. Three of the victims had been strangled, with only Yamazaki's cause of death unknown (due to her remains being nothing more than a skeleton when found). Three of the victims were from the same area of Shiroishi, with Ikegami's body dumped not far from where the four victim was located. Three of the victims were abducted and killed on a Wednesday, with only Hyakutake disappearing on a Friday night. After Hyakutake's murder, a letter was sent to her family, and after Nishiyama's murder, a letter was sent to her school. The original suspect from the first two murders would have been in his early 30s when the next two took place, making him the right age for the man (or men) witnesses saw in the reddish-brown and white cars. Were they all the same man, or different men carrying out extremely similar murders in the same area?

After Nishiyama's murder, the Wednesday Strangulations seemed to suddenly stop. The police had no solid suspects they could pin the crimes on and the case was at a standstill. Then five years later, on July 8, 1987 (Wednesday), another victim appeared.

48-year-old Fujise Sumiko lived in Kitagata City, just a few short kilometres from Shiroishi. Her husband was too ill to work, so she worked as a waitress in a Japanese inn to support their two children. Fujise left her house at 8:30 each morning, walked to work, and then usually returned home between 7 and 9 p.m. Occasionally she dropped by a nearby snack bar after her inn job to help out.

On July 8, she dropped by this snack bar with one of her colleagues to chat and eat. After they left, they stopped by another small restaurant at 9:35 p.m. Fujise invited her colleague to join her for another round, but she had to catch the train. Fujise told her that she'd also go home then (a one kilometre walk from their current location) and they said their goodbyes. This was the last anyone ever saw of her.

When Fujise hadn't returned home by midnight, her husband grew worried. The family called her colleagues to see if anyone knew of her whereabouts, but nobody had seen her. Her husband walked up and down the same route she took to work looking for her, but there was no sign. He then went to the police to report her missing. The police set out to look for her, but they also found no trace. With no body, the police couldn't be certain that foul play was at work, but considering that Fujise was the family breadwinner, it was highly unlikely that she would disappear for no reason. Still, with no body and no suspects, the case didn't get very far.

It would be another year and a half before the next victim went missing. Nakajima Kiyomi, a 50-year-old housewife, lived with her husband and daughters. The eldest daughter had already married and moved out with a child of her own, while the middle and youngest daughters still lived at home. Her husband ran a small post office that their eldest daughter also worked at, so Nakajima often took care of her grandchild while her daughter worked. They were a happy, tight-knit family with a family-run business. Despite her age, Nakajima was an extremely active woman, running her own sewing side business and participating in the local volleyball team as well.

On December 7, 1988 (Wednesday), Nakajima's middle daughter returned home for a quick break at 7:10 p.m. Nakajima had already finished dinner and was getting ready to head to volleyball practice at the Kitagata Sports Centre. She left 10 minutes later wearing an ochre sweater, striped cardigan, and navy jumper and pants. She carried 1,000 yen in her bag for her membership fees and walked to the sports centre as she always did.

It was roughly a 10-minute walk from her house to the sports centre, and she usually went with a friend, but on this day her friend had to miss training, so Nakajima went alone. One area of the route was a thin, overgrown trail that saw little traffic even during the day. Normally this would be no problem when travelling with a friend, but on this night Nakajima was alone.

Nakajima's middle daughter returned home from

work again at 10:50 p.m. Her mother still hadn't returned from training. Initially she wasn't concerned because she had heard they would be discussing what to do for the upcoming end-of-year party. Before long, however, she realised it was far too late for them to still be discussing such matters. She called the sports centre, and they revealed Nakajima had never shown up.

When Nakajima's husband got home from work, they both set out to search for her on the path towards the sports centre, but there was no sign of her. At 2 a.m. that same night, they filed a missing person's report with the Omachi police. The police and fire department set out at dawn to look for Nakajima, searching the paths leading to the sports centre and the surrounding mountains, but found nothing. Sniffer dogs were called in and they followed her scent from her house to the small trail where it abruptly ended. This trail was only five minutes from Nakajima's house. Investigations revealed one witness had seen Nakajima standing by the trail at 7:30 p.m., talking to another woman in her 30s or 40s on a bike. Police attempted to uncover who the woman was, but they were unsuccessful. As with Fujise's disappearance, the police had little to go on and the case stalled.

On January 25, 1989 (Wednesday), the final victim of the Wednesday Strangler went missing. 37-year-old Yoshino Tatsuyo worked for sewing company Rimusu, just like the third victim, Ikegami. At the time, she was living apart from her husband and back at home with her family in Kitagata. Yoshino clocked out of work at 6:55 p.m.

She got home 20 minutes later and sat down to eat dinner with her family. At 7:25 p.m. she received a brief call, only 20 seconds long, and her family heard her ask, "Where are you now? Okay," before hanging up. She finished dinner with the family and then helped wash up.

At 7:45 p.m., Yoshino got changed into a skirt and white cardigan, put on some makeup, grabbed her bag, and then jumped in her red car. As she was leaving, she informed her mother that a friend had gotten a flat tyre, so she was going to drop her off in Yamauchi, roughly 10 kilometres away. Her son, a fourth grader in elementary school, told her he wanted to come along, but she refused. As she pulled out and drove off down the street, this was the last her family ever saw of her. Later investigations revealed she didn't have any friends in Yamauchi. When she didn't return home, her father filed a missing person's report with the police, but it's unclear exactly when he did this.

Two days after Yoshino went missing, a 55-year-old housewife was driving with her husband at 5:50 p.m. when they pulled over by a small roadside altar to pray and leave offerings. The woman picked up a large branch from nearby and started gathering flowers from the roadside. She happened to look over the edge of a nearby cliff when she saw something white at the bottom. It was a cardigan. Realising it was a body, the woman quickly called the police. The body turned out to be the recently missing Yoshino, but she wasn't alone.

Two metres away they found a body wearing navy pants and a sweater. She was lying face down and her lower body was badly decomposed. It was Nakajima, who'd gone missing on her way to volleyball practice. Her cause of death was determined to be strangulation. A metre from her they discovered another body that had already turned to bones. It was Fujise, who had gone missing two years earlier. With only a skeleton to work with, the police were unable to identify her cause of death, but they verified her identity using dental records.

Various items of the women's clothing hung from trees nearby, and the branch the housewife had picked up when she got out of the car had been sawed off and placed into the ground like a marker, perhaps to remind the killer of where his victims were located. Other personal effects from the victims were discovered spread out over a two kilometre area from their corpses.

The remains of all three victims were sent for autopsies on January 28, the following day, and Yoshino's death was also determined to be from strangulation. Her mouth and nose had been blocked while she was strangled with bare hands. Judging by the state of the digested food in her stomach, this had taken place an hour after eating. Further testing discovered semen both inside Yoshino's body and on her underwear, but the state of Nakajima and Fujise's remains meant they were unable to recover anything from either of them. Testing determined the semen came from a man with type O blood, but it had been there for at least a day before she died, suggesting that she was perhaps not raped before she was killed.

Yoshino's car was found parked at Takeo Bowl bowling centre, several kilometres away, an hour and a half before her body was discovered. The doors were locked and all windows up. There were no signs of a struggle, suggesting she had parked the car there and then either walked or gotten into another car of her own free will.

A school child found her handbag on January 26, the day before, two kilometres from where her corpse was found. The child handed the bag to their grandmother, and it wasn't until later that night that they realised who it belonged to. Her car keys were found in the bag, along with a notebook, *inkan* stamp, health insurance card, handkerchief, and an empty wallet with only two yen.

Various other items belonging to Yoshino were found all over town in the following days. The police were unable to lift prints from any of them, but they determined that after the perpetrator dumped her body, he drove counter clockwise down the highway, discarding her personal effects at random along the way. Further investigations then pieced together what was likely Yoshino's final moments.

One passerby saw a woman with white clothes standing beside a red car parked at Takeo Bowl at 8 p.m. on January 25. This was only 15 minutes after Yoshino left her house, and the woman remarked that she appeared to be waiting for someone. Shortly thereafter, a man in a white Toyota Cresta arrived and picked her up. Investigations revealed there were at least 500 white Toyota Crestas registered in Saga Prefecture at the time, and 130 of those were in the Kitagata area.

Another woman reversing out of the Takeo Bowl car park around 8 p.m. that same night nearly bumped into a parked red car. The lights and engine were off, and there was no sign of anyone around. At 8:30 the next morning, the manager of Takeo Bowl noticed the red car was still parked in their lot. They didn't report the car, but the following night the police came around to investigate for themselves. One further witness, however, would come forth with information that would lead the police to a suspect they would chase for decades afterwards.

The witness worked for a fish tackle production company, and around 8 p.m. on January 25, the same time witnesses saw Yoshino getting into a white Toyota Cresta, this man saw a parked "whitish" truck in the bowling alley car park that caught his eye. It caught his eye because of a particular decoration; beneath the front window and above the driver's seat, the truck was decorated with a fish scale pattern. He wanted to ask the driver where he bought it, but there was nobody in the truck at the time. The police discovered that Yoshino's new boyfriend, Matsue Teruhiko (26 at the time), had a truck just like the one the man described, and not only that, he lived only a few hundred metres from where the three women's bodies were discovered.

The police called Matsue for questioning immediately on January 27 and kept him for four days. After being released, Matsue quit his job and moved from his family home to Fukuoka. He was then arrested in October of the same year for drug use, and while being questioned the following month, admitted that he had killed the three women.

At this point, the three Kitagata murders were being treated as a separate incident to the earlier Wednesday Strangler incidents; after all, if Matsue really was the killer, he would have only been 12 when the first victim died in 1975; not impossible, but highly unlikely. He also didn't fit the description of the man in his 30s or 40s seen with the third and fourth victims. But Matsue soon retracted his confession anyway and proclaimed his innocence. It wouldn't be the first, nor the last time that someone was forced to confess to something they hadn't done during intense police questioning, and this would later be taken into account.

It wasn't until 2002 that police finally decided to charge Matsue with the murders of the three women. The statute of limitations was rapidly approaching, meaning that if they didn't move quickly, they would lose their final chance.

Matsue, already serving time in Kagoshima Prison, was formally charged with Yoshino's murder on June 11, 2002. He was then charged with Fujise's murder on July 2, and Nakajima's murder on July 9. The statute of limitations for Fujise's murder was to end on July 7. His trial opened on October 22 and would last several years with police asking for the death penalty. But who exactly was Matsue, and why were the police so sure it was him?

Matsue was first arrested on July 20, 1984, for drug use. He served 18 months and then returned to his family home in Kitagata in 1985 on three years' probation. He helped around the family farm and worked as a driver for a concrete firm in town, but it wasn't long before he was doing drugs again.

In September 1986, Matsue got married and lived at home with his wife, mother, and younger sister. He was an abusive man and often cheated on his new bride, so it wasn't a happy home. One year later, in October 1987, he was arrested again for drugs, and on December 16 of the same year sentenced to 14 months prison. Fujise was murdered on July 8, 1986, two months before his arrest. His wife then divorced him in March of the following year while he was in prison.

Matsue was released on parole in September 1988, moved back to his family home once more and picked up his old driving job. He hooked up with an old girlfriend from before his prison time, and although they were serious, he still had other girlfriends on the side. In December of the same year, Matsue learnt that Yoshino, who he knew from around town, was moving back to her family home after splitting from her husband. He got her number and then asked her to go out with him. She accepted. It was around this time that Nakajima, the next victim, was killed.

The two soon started dating, and Matsue would call Yoshino's house to arrange where and when to meet. She would drive to the location, get into Matsue's car, and he would drive them elsewhere, usually a hotel or something similar. Yoshino's family knew nothing of this, and she would lie to them about where she was going, usually telling them that she was going to drop off a friend somewhere. Yoshino's younger sister eventually found out about Matsue's existence, but she also kept quiet about it. She knew of his truck with the fish scale decoration and was aware that he had no father and lived at home with his mother and sister. He used that same truck to deliver things for work.

At some point, Yoshino told her sister that Matsue had been threatening and violent towards her. Only days before she disappeared, Yoshino had told Matsue that it would be best if they no longer saw each other. He took her for a drive to a nearby cliff and, referencing a recent death that had taken place there, threatened her. According to later testimony from her family, Yoshino began receiving more and more calls to go out starting from December 1988 and continuing until her death. She would always finish eating, do the dishes, get dressed and then leave the house, not returning until the early hours of the morning.

Throughout January 1989, Yoshino began receiving numerous strange and threatening phone calls from someone proclaiming to be a friend of her husband. Whether this was Matsue, a friend of Matsue's, or someone else entirely, nobody knows for sure. Then, on January 23, 24, and 25—the night she went missing—Yoshino was called out three times in a row, presumably to spend time with Matsue. On January 25, she got in her car, drove to Takeo Bowl, and according to witnesses, got into a car with a man, presumably Matsue, who had parked his own truck in the same parking lot. Why would he change cars? Was it, perhaps, to hide evidence of the crime he was about to commit…?

On April 10, 2005, almost three years after the trial had begun, Matsue was found not guilty of all three murders due to lack of hard evidence. The judge also determined the signed confession Matsue made years earlier had been forced by the officer in charge and was thrown out.

Prosecutors appealed the decision, but at the first trial on March 19, 2007, the Fukuoka High Court once again ruled Matsue not guilty of the charges. Prosecutors submitted new mitochondrial evidence to the second trial, but it was determined not sufficient to secure a guilty verdict. The police were also criticised for their sloppy work on the case and for keeping the defendant locked up for so many years. On March 29, the Fukuoka Supreme Public Prosecutor's Office deemed there to be insufficient evidence to continue escalating the appeals and refused the prosecution's request to appeal further.

On April 2, 2007, Matsue was determined not guilty of the murders for the final time and released. The statute of limitations had passed on all three of the Kitagata murders, as well as the original four Wednesday Strangulations, meaning the police had no choice but the file all cases as unsolved. And while police were unable to pin the murders on Matsue, he was soon behind bars again anyway. In May 2012, Matsue was arrested for a string of 127 thefts across Kyushu and incarcerated once more.

So, who did it? Did the same perpetrator commit all seven murders, or were there multiple killers? How could so many murders in the same small area over 15 years have so many similarities, and why were there so many details the police still didn't understand? The cases are officially unsolved, but the strangeness of them has garnered much public attention over the years.

One of the most predominant theories is that there wasn't a single killer, but rather two. Two killers that the police *did* arrest and charge, but were ultimately unable to get convictions for; U, the man charged for the first two crimes but found not guilty (and who possibly killed victims three and four as well), and Matsue, charged with the final three murders but found not guilty due to a lack of evidence.

The statute of limitations has passed on all seven murders now, meaning that even if the murderer did come forth and confess, the police would be unable to do anything about it. Whether it really was the men the police charged with the crimes or not, only they know for sure, but the enduring mystery of the Wednesday Strangulations inspires debate even to this day.

Mysterious Toilet Death

At 6 p.m. on February 28, 1989, an elementary school teacher (23) from Mijakoji, Fukushima Prefecture, returned home from school and went to the toilet. When she looked down, she saw what looked like a shoe at the bottom of the pipe. This was an old-fashioned squat-type toilet, meaning she could see down the pipe to the bottom.

The woman, referred to as A, was so surprised by the sight that she ran outside and opened the lid to see what was going on. When she looked in, she saw human legs. The young teacher ran to a nearby police officer's residence and the fire department was also called in. The firefighters attempted to pull the person out of the pipe but were unable to; it was far too narrow. In the end, they were forced to dig the entire pipe out of the ground and cut it open to free the person.

Of course, the person inside was dead. Despite being the middle of winter and shockingly cold in Fukushima, the man was half naked and clutching his jacket tight against his chest. His knees were pressed up against his chest like a human cannonball, and his head tilted slightly to the left. His other shoe was eventually found on an embankment near the house.

Who was this man, and why was he jammed into a toilet pipe?

The man was revealed to be 26-year-old S. He lived in the same village with his parents and grandmother. Like many young men, he enjoyed both sports and music; he was in a band with classmates during his high school days, and he was also the senior manager of the local youth recreation club. He worked as senior operations staff of maintenance for the nuclear power plant in the next town over, and he was active in the ongoing local elections, giving campaign speeches around town. All-in-all, S was extremely active in the community and well known by most.

So, how did he end up in a 23-year-old elementary school teacher's toilet pipe?

Officially, this case has been closed. The police ruled that S died of chest circulatory disturbance in addition to the freezing cold. He had minor abrasions on his knees and elbows, but no other visible wounds or injuries, and no signs that he had been attacked. His date of death was determined as February 26, two days before his discovery. As for why he was in the pipe, police claimed that he crawled in there to peep on A, got stuck, and then froze to death. When interviewing his family, they discovered that S was in possession of lewd magazines, therefore, he must have been peeping. Naturally, people had many questions about this supposed version of events.

First of all, S was never known by those around him as the type of person who would try to peep on women. Of course, it's impossible to know what dark secrets even those closest to us may hide, but S was known as an upstanding citizen with not even a hint of such tendencies. And, supposing that S really was a peeping tom, it's difficult to fathom why he would force himself, shirtless in the freezing cold, into a toilet pipe just to catch a glimpse of someone using the toilet.

It's important to point out that the toilet pipe S was discovered in was a hard U shape and incredibly small. The opening from the outside was only 36 centimetres wide, while the opening from the toilet end was only 20 centimetres. The pipe was 107 centimetres long vertically and 125 centimetres wide horizontally. The height of the pipe at the bottom of the U was only 50 centimetres. This is the section where S was discovered, curled in the foetal position with his face beneath the toilet opening, his knees jammed against the pipe wall above him and his head and feet pushing against the walls on either side. All while holding his jacket tight against his chest.

No matter how you look at it, it was impossible for S to have squeezed into this position alone. He would have had to have gone headfirst into the pipe like a snake, holding his jacket against his chest and thus removing his arms from the equation, and then somehow bent his spine through the 36 centimetre gap to get into the bottom section of the U. The pipe wasn't curved; the corners were hard right angles. Then, if we assume he went face first, the natural way most humans would crawl into something, he would then need to turn his entire body around inside the pipe so he was then facing up; if we suppose he somehow crawled backwards into the pipe like a belly-up snake so he wouldn't need to turn around, well, that presents a whole new series of problems.

Yet despite all this, the biggest question was still "how?" How did he fit? He was jammed so tightly into the pipe that lack of circulation was said to be what killed him, and nobody was able to get him out until they cut the pipe open. Plus, let's not forget that this was a toilet pipe. People would be urinating and defecating in it, and S was—by all accounts—an intelligent man. Even if his plan was to accept a little urine and faeces to the face in exchange for getting a peep at a woman's private parts, how did he plan on getting back out of the pipe? Why didn't he just peep on her in the shower? There were too many questions, and the situation didn't make any sense.

It wasn't long before rumours began to spread about S's bizarre death. The police may have ruled it accidental, but to most that seemed like the least likely explanation, especially with a little more digging into S's background.

As mentioned earlier, S worked hard giving campaign speeches for the local election that was taking place at the time. Then, suddenly, he stopped. Why? Word had it that S had suspicions over where donation money was coming from and where it was going. When he confronted those involved, he didn't like the answers he received and so he left the campaign. In order to keep S from talking, or perhaps in a simple act of revenge, those involved in the campaign then killed him and stuffed him into the toilet pipe to hide the body. Whether we believe that he was murdered by these particular people or not, it's certainly easier to believe that S was shoved into the pipe by a third party than believing that he crawled in there by himself.

Matters were further complicated when it was later revealed that S and A knew each other, and not just in passing. The pair were acquaintances through A's boyfriend, and both men had been working together to track down someone who had been peppering A with prank calls. Thinking it a stalker, they took recordings of the calls to the police, but the police did nothing. According to a friend of S's, he had ascertained who he believed to be the culprit shortly before he died. Was this the true killer? Did whoever was hassling A discover that S was onto him, and armed with this knowledge, kill him? Then—in a twist of irony—did he hide him in A's own house, shoved painfully into the pipe beneath her toilet where he wouldn't be found until days later?

The problem with either of these scenarios is that S was discovered with only minor scratches on his body, and as mentioned earlier, he died from a combination of the cold and a lack of circulation in his chest. He wasn't killed outside the pipe and then shoved in. He died inside it. If a third party put him in there, how did they get him into such a tight space without him fighting to get away, without anyone noticing, and how did he end up in the tightly packed human cannonball position he was discovered in?

Not only that, but why was his shoe on his head and how did it get there? According to A's testimony, she saw the shoe when she looked into the toilet from inside the house. His arms were wrapped around a jacket pressed tightly to his chest with no room to move. The only possible way for the shoe to be on his head was if it was already in there and his body pushed it up as he was shoved in, or even more bizarrely, if someone dropped it into the pipe from inside the toilet. His other shoe was discovered on a bank near the house. What caused S to lose both his shoes in vastly different places?

If we look at the facts of S's death—minor abrasions on his body, death by freezing and lack of circulation—combined with the bizarreness of being stuck shirtless in a toilet pipe in winter, it's not a large jump to guess that he was unconscious before being forced in. One would assume that people would have otherwise heard his screams, not to mention those inside A's house would have undoubtedly heard a man screaming from the toilet. Yet nobody heard anything. He was there for days before being discovered. Did he never regain consciousness? Why didn't he make any noise?

All of this leads to a third, even more outlandish option: A was involved in S's death.

Although unsubstantiated, there were rumours that A was involved with delinquent gangs when she was younger. She became a teacher not by going to university, but by completing a short course at junior college and then getting hired; an extremely odd career progression. According to the rumours, she was known to still affiliate with the local (and now younger than her) delinquents, and they looked up to her as an OG. She held power and sway over them. S was active in the community, particularly with youth and other political activities, and he had been working with A at the time of his death to uncover who was bothering her.

If A was somehow connected to the political campaign that S dropped out from, or knew others involved (such as current or former gang members), then perhaps she was also involved in his disappearance as well. Perhaps the calls were a ruse to get him closer, and as he was closing in on the truth, he was attacked, knocked unconscious, stripped of all clothing but his pants and shoved into the pipe (holding his jacket, perhaps to hide that evidence as well).

If he did wake up in the pipe, his screams would likely be muffled from the outside, but audible inside; not that it would matter if A was involved. It wouldn't take long for him to die in such a cold, cramped space, and the screams would soon stop— assuming he even woke up at all. A reportedly quit her job a month after S's disappearance as well, and to make the conspiracy even more interesting, it's said that several officers involved in the case also transferred shortly thereafter…

Bizarre circumstances call for equally outlandish theories, and of course, no-one could corroborate any of this. It was all a theory, a conspiracy theory if you will, to try to fit the square pegs of the evidence into the round holes of the case. Forcing something, anything, to fit.

Even if S's death hadn't been ruled accidental by the police, the statute of limitations has long passed on this bizarre incident, so even if someone stepped forward to confess to murdering him, nothing could be done about it. More than 30 years have passed, however, so unless someone decides to confess on their death bed, we're unlikely to get any new information on this long-buried case.

Hiroshima Family Disappearance

It's not unusual for people to go missing in Japan; the past few years have seen over 80,000 people reported missing each and every year, and that number is constantly on the rise. But it's not often that an entire family disappears without a trace, leaving their home as though they'd just stepped outside to pick up the morning paper. Such was the case with one family in Hiroshima Prefecture in 2001.

In the early morning hours of June 4, 2001, the Yamagami family from the small town of Sera in Hiroshima went missing. Father Masahiro (58), his wife Junko (51), their daughter Chie (26), Masahiro's mother Mie (79), and the family's pet dog Leo all vanished without a trace. The front door to the house was locked, but the back was open. There were no signs of a struggle, nor was any blood discovered at the scene. All four family members' sandals and pyjamas were missing, and breakfast had been left on the table, suggesting the family had left suddenly. Why? Where did they go? And why did they take the dog with them?

Police initially considered that the family may have been running from money problems, but they had considerable savings, no official debts to their name, and Junko had left her bag in the house with 150,000 yen sitting inside it. She was supposed to go on a work trip to China the following day, and her packed bags were ready and waiting to go. Both her and Chie's phones and licenses were also in the house, as well as Masahiro's pager. Police discovered the lights in the kitchen and hall had been left on, and mosquito nets placed over their breakfast. The family had left in a rush; they were in their pyjamas, left the lights on, and didn't take their phones or wallets with them, but they also had enough time to cover their food and grab the family dog. The situation had police perplexed.

Interviews with neighbours revealed that the family appeared to get along well, and no-one had ever seen them arguing or fighting. What went on behind closed doors may have been an entirely different matter, but to the outside world, the family appeared happy and without problems. Masahiro came from a powerful old family, the Yamagamis, and he held considerable influence and power around town. He also worked for a rather large construction company nearby. His wife Junko worked for a quarrying company, and as mentioned earlier, was due to go on a company trip to China the following day. Both husband and wife held good jobs and were financially stable.

Daughter Chie worked as a teacher at Takehara Elementary School where she taught first graders. She was also known around town for her good looks, having won the local Miss Fruity Sera competition in 1995. She was popular with the children at school and, because of her beauty, they treated her like an idol. She didn't live with her parents, however, but in an apartment 30 kilometres away. She was unmarried, but dating a man with eyes towards marriage at the time.

The day before the family went missing, Chie attended a ball game tournament held by the school's PTA. As is the norm with most school events, she went out drinking with the other teachers afterwards, and one of them then drove her home around 9:30 p.m. Her colleague overheard Chie on the phone with her mother claiming that she'd left her makeup at their house and she would be over soon to pick it up. Chie and her colleague then parted ways, and that was the last time anyone other than her family saw her. Neighbours at the Yamagami house heard a car door slam at 10:50 p.m., which was most likely Chie's arrival to pick up her makeup.

When the newspaper delivery man dropped off the paper at 4.a.m the next morning, the family car was already gone. This meant that the family had left the house sometime between 10:50 p.m. the previous night and 4 a.m. that morning. Considering that breakfast was ready and the family's clothes for the day prepared, it was likely they left shortly before 4 a.m. rather than sometime the previous night.

The family weren't discovered missing until Junko missed the appointed meeting time for her company trip. With no word from her whatsoever, a colleague grew worried and visited the Yamagami's house, finding it in the above-mentioned state. They quickly called the police.

Where had the family gone, and why did they leave in such a hurry?

As mentioned earlier, the Yamagami family had long held influence in Sera, and had in fact owned a mountain not far from the Yamagami's house. This mountain—Taishokamiyama—had a particular legend surrounding it that people began to take more notice of once the family had disappeared. It was a rumour of *kamikakushi*, or spiriting away.

According to the legend, during the Edo Period a servant named Onatsu worked for a wealthy family who governed the area. One day, Onatsu went to visit Taishokamiyama to cut the grass. When she didn't return, however, the entire village set out to look for her. They found no trace of her; she had vanished into thin air. It wasn't long until rumours sprang up that Onatsu had been spirited away, and thereafter the mountain became famous for *kamikakushi*. Was it mere coincidence that the descendants of the family who once owned that mountain had now apparently been spirited away themselves?

At least one question was solved when on September 7, 2002, more than a year after the family had gone missing, a car was found in Kyomaru Dam, not far from the family's home. The dead bodies of all four family members and their pet dog were inside. Water levels inside the dam had dropped due to a lack of rain, which then led to the discovery of the car. Police found the car key still in the ignition and no visible signs of injury on any of the family members. There was a buffer stop in place on the road above and no way for the family to mistake where they were driving, leading the police to conclude that they had driven into the dam on purpose. It was ruled a family suicide, and the case closed. But, as with many of these cases that were officially solved, it still left more questions than answers. The biggest being: why?

This is something that nobody has been able to figure out. Why did the family—or rather, the father, Masahiro—drive into Kyomaru Dam? By all accounts, the family were happy and without problems. Junko was about to go on a work trip to China and everything was packed and ready to go. Chie was a popular elementary school teacher who had just spent the day at school taking part in various community events. Masahiro had a good job and came from a wealthy family, and his mother was well into retirement. Not only did he drive all three of the women in his life into a dam, but he took the family dog with them, too. In their pyjamas. While breakfast sat on the table at home.

The official term used by the police was *murishinjuu*. In English this translates to "forced double suicide." Meaning, not everyone was in agreement with what was going on. In these cases, usually a family member or a lover forces the other party to die with them (without their consent), or they kill their partner before taking their own life in a murder-suicide. The theory was that, for whatever reason, Masahiro killed his entire family against their will and intended to die with them. The police never announced a motive for this crime, and in the absence of an official motive, rumours quickly spread as to why.

One, of course, was money. This rumour didn't go very far because the Yamagami family were quite wealthy, and over 20 million yen was discovered in the family's term deposit account at the time of their disappearance. This idea was quickly discarded, but there was another rumour that continued to pick up steam over the years; the supposedly "true" reason why such an outwardly happy and wealthy family would suddenly disappear and turn out to have died in a family murder-suicide: infidelity.

Masahiro met Junko when they were both young and she was working as a nurse. He wanted to marry her right away, but his family strongly opposed the idea; he was heir to the family name, after all, and they viewed Junko as a mere commoner. It's the same basic plot to many a fairy tale. In the end, Masahiro eloped with Junko. He didn't return until 10 years later, after Junko had given birth to their child Chie. By that point, there was nothing the family could do. They had been married for 10 years, and now they had a child. That was how much Masahiro loved his wife and what he was willing to give up for her. He had long proven himself compulsive and willing to do whatever it was that he wanted, regardless of how others thought or felt about the situation.

If you believe the rumours, however, in the months leading up to the family's disappearance, Junko had been cheating on her husband with a colleague. This was never substantiated, of course. But word had it that her work trip to China was also doubling as an illicit trip away with a colleague she was more than a little friendly with. Her husband, unable to bear it any longer, decided that not only would he kill his wife, but he would take his own life as well. Again, this is not an uncommon concept in Japan, and it's why the word *murishinjuu* exists. If this truly were the case, however, then why did he take his mother and daughter along with them?

Masahiro's mother was old. If he planned on killing his wife and then himself, she would be left alone. Could he have placed her in a home? Definitely. The family certainly had enough money for it. But the shock may have been too much for her, not to mention the shame of having to live with her son, the heir to the Yamagami name, having killed his wife and then himself. He perhaps felt it easier to take his ageing mother with them.

But then, what about Chie? Chie was young, popular, successful, and dating with prospects of marriage herself. Why take her with the rest of the family when she didn't even live with them? Here's where things get even more outlandish.

Two years before the family went missing, the teacher's union in east Hiroshima—in particular in Sera—was in the news for "forcing" a high school principal to commit suicide, and they had apparently pushed several other teachers to take their own lives over the years as well. Reportedly, Chie was in a relationship with another teacher who was already engaged to be married, and the teacher's union was unhappy with the bad press it might bring. The man's father and other members of the union supposedly visited the Yamagami house and warned them that if Chie didn't end the relationship, then she would never work in Hiroshima as a teacher again. Many believed that this led Masahiro to grow worried about his daughter, and rather than leaving her behind to deal with the union by herself, he decided to take her along with them as well.

This was the same reason that he took the dog, too. Perhaps feeling bad for the family pet, Masahiro didn't wish to leave him behind all alone, and so decided the best course of action was to take him with them. As for how he got everyone into the car in their pyjamas so early in the morning, many theorised that he drugged their breakfast, but if he did, no evidence of it was ever found.

There was, of course, no proof for any of this, and the mysterious circumstances behind the family's deaths made the situation ripe for rumours, particularly with so many unanswered questions. The only facts that people knew for certain was that the family left the house in Masahiro's car between 10:50 p.m. and 4 a.m., the house was untouched and showed the family were getting ready for their day, and that all four family members and the pet dog were discovered a year later inside the car in Kyomaru Dam. If the police knew anything else, they weren't saying, but it doesn't make sense that they would withhold information about the case either, not when they've gone into details about far worse crimes both before and after this one.

While people have their suspicions, we may never truly know why Yamagami Masahiro and his family drove into a dam that morning, but the mysterious nature behind the case means that it will also likely never be forgotten.

Hachiouji Supermarket Robbery Murders

"Hold this urn and promise me you'll arrest the criminal this year."

1995 was a rough year for Japan, and many consider it the turning point in many of Japan's current laws against crime. The Great Hanshin earthquake shook the country on January 17, 1995, killing more than 6,000 people and throwing the country into turmoil. A few months after that, three Tokyo subway lines were attacked with sarin gas, killing 13, severely injuring 50, and causing health problems for at least 1,000 others. Only a few short weeks after that, a police chief was shot by an unknown assailant as he stepped out of his house to go to work. The criminal was never found, nor was a motive uncovered. Then, a few months after that, a crime took place that shook Japan to its core and called for widespread reform on Japan's gun laws. It's known as the Hachiouji Supermarket Robbery Murders.

Hachiouji is a large city that lies in the west of the Tokyo Metropolis area. At present it has a population just shy of 600,000 people, but that's not to say the entire city is swarming with residents. It's surrounded by the beauty of nature, and its suburbs are no different to those you might find outside of Tokyo. Many are small, cozy, and the locals are familiar with each other. Many businesses are small and run locally, as was the case with Nanpei, a tiny supermarket located in Oowada, a town in Hachiouji of 16,000 people.

On July 30, 1995, the local Bon festival was being held in a park only 60 metres from the Nanpei supermarket. It was a busy summer night with people flooding the streets to watch those performing in the parade. The festival began at 6:30 p.m. and finished at 9:15 p.m. Despite being a Sunday, the Nanpei supermarket was open. In fact, it was the final day of a three-day sale at the supermarket to coincide with the Bon festival, meaning the store had sold considerably more than usual. That money was kept in a safe on the second floor before it was transferred to a bank, meaning that safe also held considerably more money than usual. The perfect time for a robbery.

Nanpei supermarket was a small operation. Only 20 people worked there, part-timers included. One of those part-timers was Inagaki Noriko (47). Inagaki was familiar with the service industry, having managed her own bar until just a year earlier. She wanted to become an aged care worker however, so she left her job and picked up part-time work at Nanpei while she studied.

Shortly before the Bon festival, Inagaki was put in charge of caring for the safe at night. Only a select number of employees knew the code to the safe, and those on night shift were in charge of putting the day's sales into it each night and then locking it before leaving. The safe was opened by both a combination lock and a key, and the store owner would open it first thing each morning when he arrived. The safe was located in the supermarket's office on the second floor, a tiny room that also doubled as a changing room and held little else.

On the day of the Bon festival, 16-year-old Maeda Tomomi, also a part-time worker at the store, had the day off. Maeda was a bright young girl who often volunteered around the community and worked hard at school. She was close with 17-year-old Yabuki Megumi, a childhood friend who also worked part time at Nanpei with her. Yabuki was well-liked by her peers and loved children, often speaking of her desire to become a nursery school teacher in the future. Both teens were on the verge of summer holidays and already had a full agenda of things to do and friends to meet.

July 30 marked the end of Nanpei's three-day special sale. Being a busy Sunday, the supermarket was packed, and as evening approached, it grew even busier as more and more people gathered for the Bon festival. The evening shift started at 5 p.m. Yabuki arrived at 4:40 p.m. on her bicycle and shortly thereafter Inagaki arrived, driven by a male acquaintance whom she had a dinner date with after work. As the day shift filed out, Yabuki and Inagaki were the only two workers on the floor running the registers.

Shortly after 5 p.m., a suspicious man in his 50s was seen standing in front of the store by other shoppers. It was the busy day of the Bon festival, so nobody thought much of him. It should be noted that the supermarket had four security cameras in-store, but they were for monitoring only. They didn't record, and they had to be watched on the monitors upstairs. Around 6:30 p.m., the remaining workers finished their shift and left the store, leaving only Yabuki and Inagaki downstairs and the monitors unmanned.

The Bon festival also began at 6:30 p.m. at a park only 60 metres away. Thousands of people gathered to watch the singing, dancing, and drums. The town was alive with people and noise, and it was perhaps not a coincidence that the criminal chose this particular day.

At 6:50 p.m., Maeda arrived at the supermarket to check her upcoming shifts, and customers overheard her talking with Yabuki about how she would wait until her shift was over so they could attend the festival together. By 8 p.m., an hour before closing, most of the customers had filtered out and so Inagaki closed her register. Half an hour later, a strange man was again seen, this time loitering in the store without buying anything. At the same time, a local entered the supermarket to buy some ice cream before closing time and chatted with Inagaki. This customer was the last known person to see all three alive.

By this time, the Bon festival outside had reached full swing. At 9 p.m. the supermarket closed, so Yabuki closed her register. The time on the final receipt recorded this happening at 8:59 p.m. The three women made their way out of the supermarket and up to the office on the second floor. This involved leaving the store entirely, heading into the dark parking lot out back, and then up the stairs. Most of the time, this office was left unlocked during the day, and it was no different on this day either.

Money from the day's sales was placed into the

safe, then the dial spun and locked. After the supermarket's three-day sale, coinciding with the busy Bon festival, there was reportedly 5,260,000 yen inside the safe. A hefty amount for a small, local supermarket. Yabuki and Inagaki got changed out of their uniforms, and at 9:03 p.m. the drum performance began. The noise outside reached its peak. The perfect time to commit a crime.

At this same time, a suspicious man was once again seen outside the supermarket, this time in the dark parking lot beneath the office. As a car drove past and shone its headlights on him, the man reportedly moved quickly to hide his face. The driver thought nothing of it, not realising what was about to go down.

At 9:15 p.m., the drum performance ended. As it did, Inagaki called her male friend to come pick her up. This call was recorded on the phone in the office at exactly 9:15 p.m. Her friend lived only a few minutes' drive from Nanpei supermarket and told her he would be there shortly after getting ready. Two minutes later, a couple of high school students passing by heard the distinct sound of gunshots. Five in total. They weren't the only ones, and numerous people in the area reported hearing the same sounds when questioned by police. The sounds were shrugged off because the Bon festival was still in full swing—the drum performance having just ended—and many children were playing with fireworks nearby.

A few minutes later, Inagaki's male friend arrived to pick her up. Noticing the light in the office was still on, he waited for her in the parking lot. Yet 20 minutes passed and Inagaki still hadn't come down. For a moment the man wondered if Inagaki had gone on ahead to the restaurant they were supposed to eat at. Getting out of the car, he walked the 10 minutes there and looked around, but couldn't see her anywhere. At this point he grew worried, and after informing the hostess of the restaurant about what was going on, she returned to the supermarket with him.

Inagaki's final call had come from the office. The hostess climbed the stairs and found the door unlocked. Inagaki's male friend stayed back because the office doubled as a changing room, so there was a possibility that some female staff may still have been inside getting changed. The lights were on, after all. The restaurant hostess was a tiny woman, however, and there was a large counter by the door that she couldn't see over well. At this, Inagaki's friend grew even more suspicious and finally went upstairs and into the office himself. It was there that he discovered the bodies of all three women, dead.

The pair rushed to a nearby police box. Investigations revealed that only two-and-a-half minutes had passed between Inagaki's final call and when the gunshots were heard outside. In just two-and-a-half minutes, their lives had been suddenly and shockingly stolen from them. All three women were shot in the head from point blank range. They all died instantly.

Yabuki and Maeda were found lying on the floor facing each other, their hands bound together with tape. Inagaki was found slumped against the wall beside the unopened safe. The two high school girls had been shot once each in the head, while Inagaki had been shot twice in the head. Her face showed evidence she had been beaten before she died, likely with the same gun that killed her. The fifth shot was fired into the safe itself (which still had the key in it).

The gun was discovered to be a Philippine-made Squires Bingham 38 calibre revolver. It looked just like an American-made Colt, however, and many gang members at the time were unable to tell the difference, with many assuming the Squires Bingham revolver actually was a Colt. This made gathering exact information about the gun and where the criminal may have gotten it from difficult.

Various supermarkets and pachinko parlours along Japan National Route 16 had been robbed in the months leading up to July 30, and combined with the supermarket's high sales over the weekend—and the fact that the money was kept in a safe on-site—police immediately suspected this was a robbery gone wrong. But there were several strange facts that didn't neatly fit the robbery motive and confused matters.

Footprints of a single culprit were found at the scene. Only in recent years did police reveal the details of these; the man wore Japanese size 26 sneakers of a common brand that was sold countrywide in over 500 stores. Those same shoes are no longer produced today. This, combined with the eyewitness reports of a suspicious man in and around the supermarket, suggested the attack was carried out by a single person.

The footprints also led directly from the door to the safe and then back again; if the man's sole motive was robbery, why didn't he take anything from the lockers? Why didn't he take anything from the three women he had murdered? The safe was also small enough that it could have been carried away and opened at a different location. Yet not a single thing was stolen. The single bullet in the safe sure made it look like robbery was the motive, but perhaps that was deliberate.

A white Toyota was seen parked 20 metres from the store, its headlights off, as the supermarket closed at 9 p.m. Another white Toyota was then seen speeding through an intersection 30 metres from the supermarket shortly after the murders took place. A young man in his 20s wearing white clothes and a baseball cap was seen inside. Was this man the killer? Police have followed numerous leads over the years, but were unable to obtain anything solid on the white Toyota and whether the driver was involved or not.

Aside from robbery, the police also considered whether someone had a grudge against one or more of the women; in particular, 47-year-old Inagaki. Inagaki was well-regarded for both her beauty and business sense, having worked as a hostess in Tokyo for many years before opening her own bar, and at the time of her murder was studying to become an aged care worker. Before her death, Inagaki had even received a threatening letter containing a cutter knife blade that promised if things didn't change, "I'll kill you." She was officially single, but not without male companionship, and had many acquaintances all around Tokyo. One such companion was a company president who worked in Hachiouji known only as A.

A was a good friend of Inagaki's. They first met at the snack bar Inagaki ran and before long became intimate with each other. They became so close that A spent several nights a week at her house. He even claimed that Inagaki spoke to him of her troubles working at Nanpei and that security at the store was severely lacking.

"Every day they found a 10,000 yen discrepancy at the registers, and she said she was afraid," A told reporters at *Shuukan Asahi*. Money going missing from the till was just one of Inagaki's reported problems with the supermarket, and for a brief period, she quit. Yet they hassled her to come back, saying they needed her. She gave in and, according to A, the day she returned to work was the very same day the murders took place.

A didn't find out about Inagaki's death until he got home and saw it on the news. He tried to attend her funeral several days later, but there were so many people and media outlets surrounding the area that he struggled to get in. He also didn't want people to think him suspicious for hanging around, so he left. But it was too late, because A was already on the police's list of suspects.

Police found photos in Inagaki's possession of A on a trip to Hawaii. These included photos of A and his friends firing guns at a shooting range. According to A, "I went to Hawaii with some close friends and we went to a shooting range. When we returned to Japan, we all went to Nori-chan's bar to drink and look at the photos. Apparently she kept some of them, and that was how the police found out. They decided I was the criminal and came after me."

Six months after the murders, A noticed a car following him. He grew suspicious and took down its number plate, asking one of his friends at police headquarters to run it for him. It turned out to be a police car. That was how A found out he was under investigation. Annoyed, he made his way to the police headquarters in Hachiouji and told them to stop following him. If they wanted to talk to him so badly, they should come to his workplace to do so.

The very next day they did.

Two officers invited A to join them in their car and then sped down the highway, sirens blaring, before arriving at the police headquarters in Kasumigaseki and taking him to the investigation room. The very same room where police had interrogated Asahara Shoko, leader of Aum Shinrikyo and mastermind behind the Tokyo subway sarin attacks.

The police questioned him about his proficiency with guns, accusing him of often practising and claiming that he knew a lot about them. When A refuted their claims, they pulled out one of the Hawaii photos with A shooting a gun. A photo of a man shooting a gun at a range in a foreign country would hardly hold up in court as evidence, but it wasn't a good look either. Japan has always been strict on guns and many criminals would rather not use them because of the hassle involved.

Yet A had a clear alibi for the time of Inagaki's death; he was having dinner with a friend. The police refused to give up however, and even after they released him that night, they went to visit him numerous times for questioning and he became a near constant fixture at the Hachiouji and nearby Takao police stations. A claimed that the detectives told him they had spoken with yakuza members who said he was terrifying when angry, and there was no telling what he might do. They constantly brought up the photo with the gun and refused to let it go.

This went on for years, and on May 17, 2002—seven years after Inagaki was murdered—A was at work late at night when he heard a massive crash. Somebody had fired a shot through the window, shattering the glass. He alerted the police who soon found the bullet hole, but it was late so they retired for the night. More officers returned the next morning and while A worked in a separate room, he realised they were taking an extraordinarily long time. He looked outside and saw more than 10 officers standing around, and several even searched his house under the pretence of investigating the crime. A then noticed one of the detectives who had been investigating him for Inagaki's murder over the years standing outside with them. He got angry and asked him what he was doing there, but he shrugged A off and told him he was "just there to support the others." The detective then yelled to the rest that clearly they weren't going to find the gun so it was time to wrap up and go home. Even seven years after the fact, A was still being treated as a criminal and under investigation.

Police continued to involve themselves in A's life after the shooting at his workplace, and after he told them yet again that he had an alibi for the night of Inagaki's murder, they reportedly told him that it wasn't uncommon for people to "order murders." Even if they couldn't prove that he himself had shot the three women, they were apparently intent in pinning him for the crime in any way possible, even if that meant finding a way to prove that he had ordered the murders instead. Police have been accused of this many times in the past (whether rightly or wrongly is up for debate), but A felt like they didn't actually care whether he was involved or not; there was evidence to suggest he *could* have been, and they wanted to pin someone, anyone, for the crime so they could close it.

Japan has a 99% conviction rate once a crime hits the courts. Entire books have been written on the hows and whys, but needless to say, detectives are ruthless once they have their sights set on someone, and if they can get them to confess (even untruthfully), then it's case closed. Considering that the detectives had spent seven years at that point following and questioning A, they clearly didn't have enough evidence that would convict him in court, but if they could wear him down into confessing, then...

It was undeniable that A knew and was friends with members of the yakuza. Former gang members even worked for him at his company. In 2005, once such former member reportedly called his now boss and told him that he was sick and needed to go to the hospital, but he didn't have any money to do so. The man was wanted by police for questioning, so once A handed the money over, he quickly received a visit from officers himself.

"We'd like you to come down to the station today. You gave money to an acquaintance and former gang member, correct?"

A said he was unaware that his friend of more than 20 years was on the wanted list at the time, and he believed that police hoped to arrest him for "aiding and abetting the escape of a wanted criminal" and then force him into confessing to the Nanpei supermarket murders at the same time. A was taken in, fingerprinted, photographed, and even had DNA samples taken. Despite not being under arrest—officially, anyway—he was treated as a criminal and questioned over his involvement with both the wanted man and the Nanpei murders. His acquaintance eventually came forth and freed A from suspicion, but on his way out A claimed that a detective said to him, "How long do you plan on denying your involvement (in the Nanpei murders)?"

As the statute of limitations on the murders approached, A continued to find himself followed by investigators and even the mass media. At times, three or four vans waited in front of his house, waiting for him to leave so they could shove cameras in his face and question him about the murders. At the time, an article was released stating that "Z" was the last known material witness in the Nanpei murders. A asked the reporters why they assumed that he was "Z" (the letter was chosen because it was the last letter of the alphabet, just like he was the last person of interest) and discovered that the police themselves had leaked the information.

The statute of limitations for the crime was supposed to expire in July 2010, making police desperate to close the case, but that very same year the law was changed and the statute of limitations for brutal crimes such as murder was abolished. This didn't apply to crimes that had already seen their statute of limitations expire, but for those like the Hachiouji Supermarket Murders, their rapidly approaching statutes were erased and thus could remain open indefinitely. In 2013, nearly 20 years after the Nanpei murders, a detective visited A at his workplace once more. "This will be the final time," he said. "Please, come down to the station just one more time."

A agreed and during questioning discovered that the detective who had just asked him to come in was the same detective who had leaked information to the press. The pair almost came to blows before they were separated. A had been called in for questioning more than 50 times over the last 18 years, and with the statute of limitations abolished, the police showed no signs of letting up on him.

A revealed something to reporters that he hadn't told the police, however. He claimed that not long after the murders, he heard a man talking about them at a bar. He seemed to know a lot about what went down and also spoke boastfully of his skill with guns. A was annoyed that the police didn't even attempt to investigate the man, but considering that A was the only person who supposedly overheard this conversation, that's not surprising.

The man known as A was, of course, not the only suspect for these brutal murders. Police pulled a partial fingerprint from the tape used to wrap Yabuki and Maeda's hands together, but it wasn't until twenty years later that they found a possible match. Unfortunately for them, the man was already dead.

They ran the print through a database of over 10 million names and came up with a man who lived in Tama, a short distance from Hachiouji. He died ten years earlier, in his 60s, from natural causes. Particular characteristics of the fingerprints matched, leading police to believe there was a high possibility he was somehow involved, but because the prints were only partial, they weren't solid enough to be used as actual evidence. The man's DNA also didn't match that found at the scene, meaning that if it was indeed a one-man job as most suspected, it was even more unlikely that it was him. At the time of the murders, the man was involved in several robberies around the area, however, making him a suspicious figure to begin with.

Matters grew even more complicated when a Japanese member of the yakuza was arrested for selling narcotics in China and then sentenced to death. While awaiting his sentence to be carried out, the man claimed that a Chinese citizen living in Canada knew about the Hachiouji Nanpei supermarket murders. The man had led a gang of both Japanese and Chinese members who carried out robberies throughout Tokyo. Before Japanese police were allowed to interrogate the man, however, he was killed.

Police followed up on his claims and tracked the Chinese man down in Canada. Believing that he held the key to cracking the case, they had the man arrested for previous immigration law violations (he had forged Japanese passports to leave the country) and extradited back to Japan, although it took 10 years before the Canadian government agreed and sent him back.

Despite intense questioning, the man never gave anything up. He was a prime suspect; the man had worked various jobs in Japan around the time the murders took place, including at an ironworks, and iron powder was found in the criminal's footprints in the office. And yet despite all this, the man claimed he would rather spend the rest of his life in jail than talk, and he remained silent until the end. After serving two-and-a-half years in prison for violating immigration laws, and without saying a word on the Nanpei murders, he was sent back to Canada.

Although the murderer was clearly familiar with guns—the location and trajectory of the bullets that killed all three women showed a skilled and calm hand—the fact that the man left behind a fingerprint on the tape indicated to police that the man did not fear them finding it. A strong possibility for this was because the murderer had no previous convictions, and thus no fingerprints in the database to compare to. It was highly unlikely that the murders were the criminal's first, but he was also skilled enough that he hadn't been caught yet. It's hard to deny this, because to this day he still hasn't been caught, despite a healthy list of suspects over the years and more technologically advanced investigation methods.

Or, perhaps, the police were looking in the wrong place. Before she died, Inagaki was said to have had a few run-ins with a local religious group. As you may recall, this was the same time period Aum Shinrikyo was poisoning Tokyo's subways and planning numerous other attacks around Japan, and they were, of course, not the only cult around. If robbery wasn't the motive, as many suspected it wasn't, then that meant the brutal murders were personal in nature. Almost everyone agrees that Yabuki and Maeda were unfortunate collateral damage—simply in the wrong place at the wrong time—and if the crime was a personal vendetta, then it was against Inagaki. Inagaki was the only one to receive two shots to the head, and with her history of running a snack bar, had associated with various shady figures over the years.

Wilder theories, spurred by the police's interest in the Chinese man, suggested that the Chinese mafia were responsible for the murders. It would explain why the killer had no fear of leaving his fingerprint behind (no previous convictions in Japan), the trained hand that killed all three women in such a short period of time, and the police's inability to find the killer after (he returned to China). The Japanese yakuza member arrested and then killed in China (who then pointed the finger to the Chinese man living in Canada) helped lend credence to the wild theory, but at the end of the day, it was just that. It also left one massive question hanging: why? Why would the Chinese mafia need to target a 47-year-old Japanese woman who was in training to be an aged care worker? What was so bad in her past—that police couldn't dig up—that would require an international crime syndicate to put a hit on her?

For all the focus on Inagaki and how the crime may have been perpetrated by someone out to get her, little has been said about how the death of the two high school students affected the lives of those around them. Their deaths were so sudden and so brutal that many couldn't believe it at first, including their high school teacher Ito Takahisa. Ito fell into a state of shock after receiving news of the death of two of his students, and according to Ito himself, it was Yabuki and Maeda's classmates who managed to bring him back.

"They told me to pull myself together," Ito told reporters. He couldn't continue to be a teacher in such a state, but rather than trying to forget the murders had happened and moving on, both Ito and his remaining students organised a school festival to think about the effect guns had on people's lives. Students wrote and presented reports on gun crimes, and then a memorial was held for the two students who had been senselessly murdered by one. They worked together to bring light to the crime and further highlight the destructive power of guns, but while they were able to eventually move on with their lives, many were dissatisfied at how the case seemed to be going nowhere.

The police have been criticised numerous times over the years for their poor handling of the case. The initial investigation was sloppy, with vital evidence such as the fingerprint ruined because of careless handling. The investigator in charge of the case was also changed partway through, setting the case back, and it has taken more than 20 years for police to uncover vital pieces of information, long after it might have been useful. There were even claims that the police let a vital suspect go immediately after the murders because he "didn't seem suspicious."

Whoever the criminal was, he had knowledge of the supermarket's security measures and after-hours handling of money. His actions indicated he knew that the person on night shift would carry the day's sales outside and up the stairs to the second-floor office, where it would then be placed in the safe. He perhaps did not expect Yabuki and Maeda to still be around, as he bound them together with tape to keep them out of the way. What remains unclear to this day is whether the attack was a simple robbery gone wrong, or whether it was a personal vendetta against Inagaki that Yabuki and Maeda were unfortunately dragged into for being in the wrong place at the wrong time.

In July 2006, a 30 million yen reward was offered for information leading to the capture of the Nanpei supermarket killer. Another 30 million yen was then added for a total of 60 million. The case is still open, and the Metropolitan Police Department still has a page up looking for information that might help them solve the case. In particular, they are looking for a couple who were the last people who bought something from the store only 20 minutes before the three women were murdered. The man is described as being 177 centimetres tall, while the woman had shoulder-length hair and was wearing a black dress. Their receipt was time-stamped as 8:56 p.m., the final transaction of the day.

Nanpei supermarket in Hachiouji no longer exists. The building was torn down after the murders and is now a parking lot. A sign was erected in front of the lot detailing the crime and asking for anyone with information to call the police. It still stands on the lot to this day.

Numerous suspects have been looked at over the years, with perhaps the strongest suspect slipping through the cracks because he's no longer in the country and refused to talk when he was. Yet more than 20 years after the brutal murders took place, people still bring the crime up as an example of a horrific gun crime that shook the country. Was it robbery, or was it personal? Why were three lives so brutally snuffed out seemingly for nothing? Sadly, we may never know.

Paraquat Serial Poisoning Incidents

The 1980s were a different time. People were more trusting, news took more time to travel, and the technology we take for granted now was far less prevalent. Thanks to all of these factors, the mid-80s saw a string of incidents take place across Japan known as the Paraquat Serial Poisoning Incidents.

From April 1985 to December of the same year, 34 poisoning incidents occurred at vending machines across the country. Of those, 13 people died, numerous people were arrested for copycat crimes, and several others were arrested for poisoning themselves and claiming they were victims. The real criminal was never found, and the case remains unsolved to this day.

The first victim turned up on April 30 in Fukuyama City, Hiroshima Prefecture. A truck driver stopped to pick up a drink and noticed a bottle of Oronamin C—a vitamin drink—sitting on top of the vending machine. Either failing to notice or not caring that the seal was broken, the man finished the drink. He soon started vomiting and was hospitalised before dying on May 2. Paraquat, a common herbicide available over the counter, was found in his vomit and determined to be the cause of death.

For several months, things fell quiet. It could have been the lone incident of a disturbed mind, but it was just the beginning. On July 11, a 48-year-old man from Fukuchiyama in Kyoto died after drinking a drink mixed with paraquat. Officially police ruled this death a suicide, but it bore an uncanny resemblance to the truck driver's death in Hiroshima (several prefectures away). Again things fell quiet, but September was about to see an explosion of incidents all around the country.

On September 11 in Izumisano, Osaka, a 52-year-old man on his way home from fishing stopped by a vending machine and picked up a bottle of Oronamin C. As he bent down to remove it from the bottom of the machine, he noticed another bottle was already sitting inside. He took both bottles home and drank them. He died three days later. Paraquat was discovered inside one of the empty bottles.

The day after the fisherman bought his drinks in Osaka, a 22-year-old university student in Matsusaka, Mie Prefecture, bought a bottle of Real Gold. Noticing another bottle already in the bottom of the vending machine, the student took both home, just like the fisherman. They died two days later, but this time diquat was found in one of the empty bottles (the only case where the poison wasn't paraquat).

By this point, the killings had made the news in Japan and people were warned not to drink anything if the seal had been broken. Although it seems like common sense to us now, seals on drinks weren't commonplace until another similar incident took place in 1977. In this case, a 16-year-old high school student picked up a bottle of cola on his way home from his part-time job. He took it home, drank it, and soon after noticing that the drink tasted strange, began throwing up. He was taken to the hospital and had his stomach pumped, but they were unable to save him. Cyanide was discovered in the cola bottle.

Several incidents of cyanide poisoning continued to take place through Tokyo, eventually killing three people. Nobody was ever charged, but as a result, the recyclable bottles that were used to sell drinks were changed to the sealed bottles and cans we still use today. Once opened, the seal breaks and there is visible evidence that the drink has been opened. But even in 1985, many people either failed to notice or care about the seals, and being more trusting than we are today, thought little about taking a full drink home, even if it had already been opened.

Police did their best to advise people not to drink anything they found that had already been opened, but news was slow to travel and, unlike the cyanide cola poisonings that took place in big city Tokyo, most of the paraquat poisonings took place in the smaller outer suburbs of cities far from the capital. Many of the victims were elderly; products of a more trusting generation that never had to worry about mass indiscriminate poisonings.

On September 19, a 30-year-old man from Fukui Prefecture picked up a bottle of cola sitting at the bottom of a vending machine. He began to feel unwell after drinking it and passed away three days later. Paraquat was discovered both in the remains of the cola and his pumped stomach contents. A day after that, a 45-year-old man from Miyazaki Prefecture found a bottle of Real Gold sitting in the bottom of the vending machine after purchasing his own. He drank both after returning home and then died two days later. Once again, paraquat was discovered in one of the drinks.

On September 23, a 50-year-old man from Osaka bought a bottle of Oronamin C and found another already sitting in the bottom of the vending machine when he went to pick it up. He didn't drink these until two days later, and the day after that, complained of feeling ill. He died on October 7.

These poisonings were taking place all over the country. If it was the work of a single person, they must have been doing an incredible amount of travelling. The police were at a loss as to who it may have been and what their motive was. Nobody stepped forward to claim it was them. The attacks were indiscriminate, leaving the bottles in or around vending machines for anyone to pick up. There seemed to be no rhyme or reason to it. And if it wasn't one person, that meant several other people out there had heard the news and decided to poison drinks in the same manner themselves. Why? What did anyone have to gain from this? This was a time before surveillance cameras, so investigations struggled to turn up anything.

As the paraquat poisonings were taking place at vending machines all around the country, several copycat crimes were also taking place around Tokyo. On September 17, an art gallery worker poisoned the coffee she gave her boss and a fellow colleague. The woman had been embezzling money from the gallery and feared discovery. Both men survived and the woman was arrested, but unlike the paraquat poisonings, the woman instead used hydrocyanic acid.

On September 25, a university student went to the police and complained that a drink he bought tasted funny. Testing found lime sulfur. The crime went unsolved. Two days later, a 44-year-old woman picked up a drink from a vending machine and, after realising that it tasted funny, also went to the police. This drink was also found to have lime sulfur in it. Again no criminal was found.

On the same day, a junior high school student in Osaka also complained to police that his drink tasted funny. Investigations revealed the boy had poisoned himself with pesticide. When asked why, he revealed that he thought he would get sympathy from his classmates if they thought he was one of the victims of the paraquat poisonings, so he did it to himself. Three days later, a 22-year-old in Fukui also went to the police complaining that his drink tasted strange. As with the high school boy in Osaka, the police found that the man had poisoned himself with pesticide and arrested him.

The paraquat poisonings didn't stop there. Throughout October, another four victims died from tampered drinks they had bought or picked up at vending machines, and another two died in November. The final confirmed victim of the paraquat poisonings was a 17-year-old high school student from Saitama who, like many of the victims, bought a drink and found another already sitting at the bottom of the vending machine when she went to take it out. She died a week after drinking it. It should be noted that, by this point, many vending machines across the country had put up signs warning people not to drink any cans or bottles they found open. This high school girl was the thirteenth person to die since April, and still nobody knew who was doing it or why.

Yet she was not the last person to die. Although the high school student from Saitama was the final confirmed victim, one more person died on December 11, a few weeks later, in Gunma Prefecture. This death, however, was ruled a suicide. A junior high school student bought a drink from a vending machine, took it home, and put paraquat in it himself, taking his own life. With his death, the paraquat poisonings that had been taking place all over the country for several months suddenly ceased. As the poisonings stopped, so did the investigation progress. Nobody was ever brought forward as a suspect, and the police were at a complete loss.

The case shook Japan for its cruel and indiscriminate nature. The trusting people of the countryside were forced to be more suspicious of their surroundings, and if the 1977 cola poisonings weren't enough to make people aware of the dangers of food and drink tampering, the paraquat poisonings of 1985 certainly did. Counteracting paraquat once it enters the body is also extremely difficult, so people soon clamoured to have the sale of it banned. It wasn't until 1999 that all sales of paraquat were banned, however, and it's no longer available for sale anywhere in Japan. But as for who poisoned all those people in 1985, and perhaps more importantly, why, it still remains a mystery to this day.

Nagoya Pregnancy Slashing Incident

On March 18, 1988, an office worker arrived home to a sight that most couldn't imagine in their wildest dreams. His heavily pregnant wife lay dead on the floor of their apartment, their baby cut from her stomach and lying on the floor beside her.

The baby was still alive.

Moriya Mitsuko (27) was several days past her expected delivery date. Heavily pregnant, she remained at home while her husband (31, unnamed in the press but often referred to as S) went to work. He called her from work each day to check how she was doing, and on March 18 he called her as usual at 1:10 p.m. to check on her. She sounded happy and energetic when she answered. He called again at 6:50 p.m., just before he was about to leave work, but this time there was no answer. He called back several times, growing more and more worried when no-one picked up.

S left work just after 7 p.m., then took the train to Toda Station, a five-minute walk from their apartment. The entire trip took roughly 30 minutes. When he reached the front door, he found it unlocked; odd, because it was always locked, even when his wife was home. The apartment was pitch black; again, strange, because it was dark outside and his wife should have been home. She was ready to give birth at any moment, so she couldn't go very far. S got changed out of his work suit, but things grew even stranger, and immediately more worrisome, when he then heard something unexpected: the sound of a crying baby.

Turning the lights on, S discovered his wife lying on the ground in her blue maternity dress and their newborn son lying on the floor between her feet. The boy was alive and crying, his umbilical cord cut. At first he thought that his wife had given birth to the child at home, but then he realised that she wasn't moving, and not only was she not moving, but her hands were tied behind her back. The power cord from the family's *kotatsu* (heated table) was also wrapped around her neck, and it was then that he noticed the blood all over the floor. He knelt down to check his wife, but she was no longer breathing.

S rushed to find the phone to call the police, but it was nowhere to be found; the cord had been torn out of the wall. Panicking, he ran to the neighbours downstairs and borrowed their phone instead. Police received his phone call at 7:43 p.m. He then rushed back upstairs, picked up the baby, and as he was cleaning the blood from it, he noticed something strange yet again. His wife's stomach appeared oddly shaped. Looking closer, he saw that it had been cut open with a 38 centimetre long and 2.8 centimetre deep gash, but that wasn't the worst part; inside he found the missing phone and his wife's car keys with a Mickey Mouse key chain attached.

Needless to say, S was both shocked and horrified. Only a few hours earlier he had spoken to his wife on the phone. She sounded happy and fine. Now that same phone was, for some inexplicable reason, shoved into her open womb—alongside her car keys—and their baby son had been cut free. Who could do such a thing, and why?

Police rushed to the scene, and the baby was taken to hospital. He had cuts to the back of his thighs and knees, hypothermia, and anaemia. He was also suffering from cyanosis (discolouration of the skin due to low oxygen). The newborn underwent an hour-long surgery and was eventually discharged on April 2 with a clean bill of health. The mother Mitsuko, however, was dead, killed in a manner that baffled both the police and the public.

Mitsuko's cause of death was determined to be strangulation by the kotatsu cord. Judging by her stomach contents, this had taken place shortly after 3 p.m., just two hours after her husband had last spoken with her. There were no signs of sexual assault, and the child was cut from her womb after her death. There were also signs the murderer had washed his hands clean of blood in the kitchen sink, and all fingerprints in the house had been wiped clean.

Police honed in on S as their initial suspect. Despite the horrifying scene he had been greeted with on his arrival home, two things struck the police as odd. First, he got changed out of his suit before looking for his wife. Despite the door being unlocked and the apartment dark, the first thing he did when he got home was get changed out of his clothes. He didn't immediately look around the apartment for his wife. Second, he appeared "too calm" in front of the press when speaking of his dead wife. He appeared before the media after her funeral and said, "My wife enjoyed wine, so please pour some out for her." He then poured some red wine in dedication to his wife for all to see. To the police, this seemed more like a performance than a husband's genuine reaction to the death of the woman he loved.

Yet, regardless of the police's suspicions, S had an air-tight alibi; he was at work when his wife died. People grieve in their own ways, and there's no telling how anyone would react to the state Moriya's husband found her and their newborn child in. As for getting changed before looking for his wife, again, nobody knows what state of mind he was in when he arrived home to such strange circumstances, nor the type of day he might have had. Japanese offices are stressful places to work; it's not impossible to think he may have wanted to get out of his work clothes as soon as possible. How could he have even imagined the situation waiting for him in the living room? Neither of these things make the man a murderer. At best, perhaps, somewhat careless and unsure of how to handle his wife's very public and very brutal death.

Mitsuko and her husband ran a side business from their apartment selling health, beauty, and home care products for Amway. On the day of her murder, Mitsuko sold some deodorant to a friend who visited their house at 1:50 p.m. to pick it up and have a chat. It wasn't uncommon for people to visit their apartment to pay for and pick up their goods at various times of the day. For a while, the police suspected the killer may have been a jealous rival, but they were unable to find any concrete evidence.

What they did find was that at 3 p.m. on the day Mitsuko died, a suspicious man was seen loitering in front of the Moriya's apartment building. The housewife living on the first floor heard someone rattling doorknobs at 3:10 p.m. before her doorbell went off. When she answered, a short man in his 30s wearing a black jacket asked, "Do you know where Nakamura-san lives?" The woman didn't know anyone by the name and told the man as such. He left, and she closed the door. Numerous other witnesses also saw the same man standing around the apartment building around 3 p.m. The same time Mitsuko was killed.

Mitsuko went downstairs to the parking lot with her friend at roughly 3 p.m.; the same time the man was seen loitering. She left the door unlocked as she did because she was just seeing her friend off. It's possible that this man saw her leave and took the opportunity to sneak into her house while the door was open. When he attempted to get into the house downstairs, he didn't first ring the doorbell; he jiggled the doorknob to see if it was open and then, after making some noise, rang the bell. Was the man simply looking for an opportunity to get into an apartment, any apartment, at random?

When Mitsuko's friend came to visit, she brought some strawberries with her which they shared as they chatted. When her husband discovered her dead body that night, the empty dishes were still sitting on the kotatsu. Taking her time of death into consideration, along with the sightings of the suspicious man outside (both a short time after 3 p.m.), it's likely that Mitsuko was attacked shortly after returning to the apartment from seeing her friend off. Her wallet with the

2,000 yen she received from her friend was taken, but nothing else in the apartment was touched, so robbery was not considered the main motive for the crime.

People living in nearby apartments reported they didn't hear any screaming or sounds of a scuffle around the time Mitsuko was killed. It's likely the man surprised her as she entered the house and then choked her to death before she knew what was going on, and in her heavily pregnant state, she was unable to fight back. However, when Mitsuko's body was found with the kotatsu cord wrapped around her neck, it was still plugged into the wall. This has led some to believe that Mitsuko was first killed with another weapon (such as the knife that was used to cut her baby out) and then the cord was wrapped around her neck after to confuse matters. It's also possible that the killer plugged the cord back in after choking her because he wanted to confuse police, or maybe just for the hell of it. The man placed the household phone and the woman's car keys inside her freshly cut womb, so plugging a cord back in would have been the least of his bizarre actions.

No knife was found at the scene of the crime, and the clean cut of Mitsuko's womb (plus the fact that the baby's umbilical cord had been cut) suggested that the man worked in the medical field. However, further investigations revealed that the man had made two or three attempts in the same spot before he finally cut through to the womb, and the medical procedure for C-sections at the time was to cut from the bellybutton down, whereas the man had cut up to her bellybutton instead. The man may have been involved in the medical field, but he wasn't fully familiar with C-section procedures. Was the man a hobbyist with an interest in medicine, someone who worked in a related field, or a doctor who wanted to throw the scent off by deliberately doing things in a non-standard way?

To make matters more confusing, a white car was seen parked in the apartment building's car park between 2 to 3 p.m. with its engine running. Then, at 3:10 p.m., a stocky man wearing a coat was seen running north from the building. He turned left at an intersection 50 metres from the building and then disappeared. Shortly after this, the short man in the black jacket rang the doorbell of the housewife living on the first floor and asked if she knew where Nakamura-san lived. He had apparently been asking people all along the road from Toda Station the same question. Then, around 4:30 p.m., another man was seen loitering in the area wearing a beret and coat with the collar up to hide his face.

There's no way to confirm whether any of these men knew each other, or if any (or all) were involved in Mitsuko's murder. Police investigations turned up nothing on the identities of all three, nor could any concrete evidence tie any of them to the crime.

Numerous theories have been suggested over the years as to the motive of the strange murder. The phone receiver and car keys being inserted into the woman's womb after death has led some to believe that the crime was the handiwork of a business rival. Both the phone and car were important to the couple's side business and they would be unable to work without either, and they were reportedly doing quite well at the time of Mitsuko's murder. On the other hand, Mitsuko's husband would need a phone to call the police upon discovering her body, or a car to drive to the nearest police station. By hiding both of those inside the dead woman's womb—a place most people would never imagine looking, or want to put their hands in if they knew—the killer could slow the arrival of the police.

It's hard to ignore the suspicious man seen by many rattling doorknobs, looking into houses, and asking for "Nakamura-san." Some have suggested that this mysterious "Nakamura-san" may not have really existed and was just an excuse for the man if people questioned his suspicious behaviour. If that was so, then why did he deliberately ring doorbells up and down the street? Why not just look for a house that had its door unlocked and freely enter?

Another theory is that the man was looking for someone to kill. Someone that matched his "type." It was 3 p.m. on a Friday afternoon. The only people likely to be home would be housewives and/or their children. By ringing doorbells, the man would get a good look at who lived inside and see if anyone else was with them. He could judge the situation at a glance while simultaneously looking for someone that matched his type.

It's also possible that he was actively looking for a pregnant woman, and there's no telling how long he may have been searching until he came across Mitsuko; a young woman described by many as beautiful. The steady yet slightly amateurish hand that cut open her womb may have indicated his motive all along: finding a pregnant woman so he could cut her baby out. As bizarre as it sounds, it still wouldn't be the strangest motive for a crime.

Or perhaps cutting the baby out was a final act of "compassion," perhaps a sliver of guilt for killing a woman clearly ready to give birth. However, the man then placed the baby on the ground and left him there for hours before anyone returned home to find him. Doctors were able to save the boy's life, but any slower and it may have been too late.

The statute of limitations for the crime passed in 2003 without any solid suspects. Shortly after her murder, Mitsuko's husband and their son moved to Saitama to be near her parents and start anew. However, everyone knew of the crime due to its bizarre and violent nature, and in 1999, S and his son moved overseas to get away from it all. At least publicly, no-one has heard from them since.

Setagaya Family Murder

Some crimes are so brutal, so heinous, that they cause a country to reform its laws. The Setagaya Family Murder was one such crime.

Setagaya is a ward of Tokyo. It's the second largest in area, yet the largest in population with over 900,000 people residing in an area almost 60 kilometres square. It's a busy area, with one of the highest residential populations in all of Tokyo. And in 2000, it was home to a bizarre, brutal murder that shook Japan to its core. On December 30, 2000, an entire family was violently killed in their home. The killer has never been found.

Entire books have been written about what happened that fateful night. The brutal nature of the murders, combined with the killer's strange actions after have long been the subject of discussion and debate. The killer left so much evidence behind that police informed the public that they would soon wrap the case up, and yet to this day, they still have no idea who did it, or why.

Shortly after 11 p.m. on December 30, only an hour before New Year's Eve, one of the biggest holidays in the Japanese calendar, a man climbed into a window on the second floor of the Miyazawa household. The family consisted of father Mikio (44), mother Yasuko (41), their daughter Niina (8) and son Rei (6). Mikio worked for a consulting agency while Yasuko ran a private cram school from their home. Yasuko's mother lived in the house next door.

The Miyazawa house had a rather unique

construction. The first floor consisted almost entirely of a study; Mikio used this for his work and the children for school. The family had a computer hooked up to the internet (not extremely common at the time, but not rare either) that faced a wall of bookshelves. Stairs at the end of this room led to the second floor which held most of the normal household features; toilet, bathroom, kitchen, living room, as well as the children's room which took up the majority of space. It's believed the criminal entered the house through the bathroom window by climbing a tree located in the immediately adjacent Soshigaya Park (only a few centimetres and a small fence separated the house from the park). A ladder then led to a third-floor loft which the parents used as a bedroom. This loft was only 170 centimetres high. A garage was attached to the study on the first floor, but police found no evidence the killer had ever entered it, and it was shut the entire time.

The killer's footprints were found directly beneath the bathroom window on the second floor, which was open and the screen covering removed. The tree in Soshigaya Park directly beneath the window also had a broken branch, leading investigators to believe this was how the man gained access to the house. This would not have been a particularly taxing way to get in, especially for someone young and fit. The front door was locked at the time of discovery with no sign of the killer's fingerprints, further solidifying the theory. Some, however, have argued that the criminal *did* enter through the front door. No fibres from the man's jumper were discovered on the bathroom window (which would have been likely if he squeezed through that way), and bloody footprints in the house were only found going up the stairs, not down. This, however, contradicts the version of events police believe took place.

All four victims died around 11:30 p.m., according to testing done on their stomach contents. The killer first approached 6-year-old Rei sleeping in bunk beds near the second-floor bathroom. Yasuko and 8-year-old Niina were asleep in the loft at the time, and Mikio was working in the study downstairs. The killer strangled Rei as he lay asleep in bed. The boy woke and kicked up a fuss, alerting his father downstairs. Mikio ran upstairs and attacked the intruder, but in the struggle was stabbed in the head with a sashimi knife. The attack was so violent that part of the blade snapped off in his skull. Mikio's body was found at the bottom of the stairs, indicating that he fell during the scuffle or was pushed.

The killer then entered the loft with the broken remains of the sashimi knife. He stabbed both Yasuko and 8-year-old Niina numerous times as they slept. Yasuko and Niina's blood was discovered on the bed on the third floor, yet their bodies were discovered on the second floor. It appeared that the pair fled during the brutal attack and the killer continued the assault with a knife taken from the nearby kitchen. Yasuko and Niina died at the top of the stairs leading to the first floor.

It's been noted that the killer used different methods for killing depending on the sex of his victim. 6-year-old Rei was choked to death with the killer's bare hands, yet other than a trickle of blood coming out of his nose from the asphyxiation, police couldn't find any other wounds on the boy. Mikio, who ran upstairs after hearing the disturbance, was found with slashes to his thighs and buttocks before the knife to the head killed him. Yasuko and Niina, however, faced far more brutal deaths.

Police found numerous lacerations to their heads, faces, and necks as the killer stabbed them from above while they slept. Yasuko and her daughter were stabbed repeatedly and violently, and police found evidence that the killer continued stabbing them long after death as well. Bloodied tissues with Niina's blood were discovered at the scene which police believed Yasuko may have used to tend to her daughter's wounds before the attack continued once more. Wounds on Yasuko's face indicated the killer attempted to gouge her flesh out as he stabbed her. Their bodies were left lying on the ground where they died, while Rei was turned face down on the bottom bunk bed and covered with a blanket.

Neighbours claimed to hear sounds of a struggle sometime after 11 p.m., and Yasuko's mother, who lived next door, heard a loud bang around 11:30 p.m. She thought it was the loft ladder being put away for the night and nothing more, but when she called the family the next morning and received no answer, she grew worried. Yasuko's mother went over to their house at 10:40 a.m. and knocked on the door. When she still got no response she used a duplicate key to enter and discovered her son-in-law dead at the foot of the stairs, and her daughter and grandchildren dead on the second floor.

The violent nature of the crime, particularly against the 8- and 6-year-old children, shook the country. New Year's is a time for family—one of the most important holidays in the Japanese year—and in a span of 30 minutes an entire family had been brutally murdered in their own home. But that wasn't where the strangeness stopped. The killer's movements after the crime have been the subject of discussion and confusion for 20 years now.

After killing the Miyazawa family, the killer remained in their house for several hours, leaving sometime before 10 a.m. the next day. The killer injured his right hand while fighting the family, which he treated at the scene. After finding the family's first aid kit, he left fingerprints on the box, some adhesive plaster, as well as blood on a towel and various other places around the house. The killer was determined to have type A blood, which none of the Miyazawa family members had. At some point the killer removed the bloodied plaster and stuck it to the back of a notebook in the living room. There was also evidence he tried using Yasuko's sanitary pads to stop the bleeding, leaving them lying around covered in his blood.

The killer then helped himself to the family's fridge. He took out a bottle of barley tea, a melon, and at least four single-serve tubs of ice cream. One empty tub was found in the bathroom, another on a cushion in the living room, and two more by the computer on the first floor. Another half-eaten tub was discovered on the rice cooker in the kitchen, but it's uncertain whether it was the killer's or left by a family member. A cup the killer used to drink the barley tea from was also discovered in the kitchen with the killer's saliva on it. At some point, he also chewed gum as he searched the house.

The fridge was full of beer and cola, which the criminal didn't touch. On top of the fact that no drugs or alcohol were discovered in his system at the time of the murders, this led police to believe that the killer was a non-drinker. Chances were high that the man was young, fit, and healthy, but it was also impossible to rule out that the man was abstaining from alcohol at the time of the crime so his judgement would not be impeded.

The family's credit cards, driver's licenses, and other cards with identifying information on them were found scattered on and around the sofa on the second floor. The drawers in the cupboards and desks had also been searched one by one from the bottom up, a method particular to cat burglars. In the bathroom, police found the father's business papers and receipts, worksheets from the mother's cram school, as well as her pads that had been used to stop the killer's bleeding, the bloody towel, and another ice cream cup. Police believe the man was disregarding items he no longer wanted or needed by disposing of them in the bathroom. More bizarrely, police also found advertising leaflets from the mail had been carried to the bathroom and cut with scissors or torn apart by hand.

The criminal made himself so at home that he even used the family's toilet. Police were able to test some of the excrement left behind and discovered that the killer had eaten beans, vegetables, and *goma-ae* (a type of salad with sesame dressing) beforehand. This differed to the contents of the family's stomachs at their time of death. At some point, he even took a nap on the family's sofa as their dead bodies lay nearby.

The killer also used the family's PC on the first floor. Analysis of the computer revealed someone (likely Mikio) using the computer between 10:20 and 10:50 that night, immediately before the murders. The computer was then turned off at 10:50 p.m. However, it then recorded connecting to the internet twice after the family was killed; once at 1:18 a.m. and again at 10:05 a.m., only 30 minutes before Yasuko's mother entered the house.

For years police believed that the killer stayed inside the Miyazawa's house for nearly 12 hours before fleeing shortly before Yasuko's mother arrived, however, in 2014, they revealed that extensive testing had shown the computer connected to the internet automatically if the mouse was bumped or impacted. The second time it connected to the internet, it recorded accessing Mikio's company work page for four minutes and 16 seconds; this was the browser's homepage, meaning that it was likely something bumped the mouse and it automatically connected to the internet at this time. What caused this to happen is unknown.

What makes matters more confusing is that the computer was unplugged when police arrived. Meaning that between 10:10 a.m. and 10:40 a.m., when Yasuko's mother arrived, someone unplugged it. The police found the killer's fingerprints on the mouse but not on the keyboard, meaning he likely perused the internet briefly before moving on. He was recorded as using the internet for only five minutes and 18 seconds at 1:18 a.m. He accessed the website for the Shiki Theatre Company (one of Japan's largest and best-known theatre companies) and created a new empty folder. Police considered whether any of this had also been done automatically, but the computer recorded that the website was browsed, the killer's fingerprints were found on the mouse, and the plug had been physically removed from the wall, all of which meant he had interacted with the computer at least briefly.

The most confusing part was the access at 10:05 a.m. Even if the internet connected automatically after the mouse was bumped, something had to bump the mouse in the first place, and the power cord couldn't exactly pull itself out of the wall either. This strongly indicated the killer *was* still in the house almost a full 12 hours after murdering the family.

The most prevailing theory is that the killer left the house between 10:10 a.m. and 10:40 a.m. Yasuko's mother alerted police at 10:56 a.m. on December 31, 2000. A passerby reported the Miyazawa's lights were off when they passed by in the early hours of December 31, but it's possible that the killer left them off deliberately so as not to attract attention.

Police were unable to determine where the killer ran after leaving the house. The Miyazawa's house was located close to numerous train stations and bus stops, and a path nearby ran along the Sen River, which itself led to a national highway and then even more train stations. However, that same afternoon, police received reports of a man on the high-speed train arriving at Tobu-Nikko Station at 5:26 p.m. with "a wound on his right hand deep enough to see the bone." The train left from Asakusa Station in Tokyo, while Tobu-Nikko is in Tochigi Prefecture to the north. If this was the killer, then he was getting as far away from the scene as he could.

The man received treatment for his wound at the station office. Described as being in his 30s and 175 centimetres tall, the man was wearing jeans and a black down jacket. He never gave station attendants his name nor a reason for his injury. Further complicating matters, police were slow to follow up on the lead, initially believing that the killer had fled during the night and not mid-morning. By the time they did, it was already too late. The man was long gone. It would have been easy for the man to reach Asakusa Station from numerous stations surrounding the Miyazawa's house, but the delay in police following up the tip meant that, to this day, they still have no idea who the man was or where he went after leaving the station in Tochigi Prefecture.

Police discovered several of the items left behind by the killer were sold in the areas around the Ogikubo (Tokyo) and Hon-Atsugi (Kanagawa) Stations, indicating that he may have spent a lot of time in those areas, either for work or residence. The man left a surprising amount of personal items behind, which initially led police to believe that solving the case would be easy.

They were sorely mistaken.

On the second floor, they found a sweatshirt, the sashimi knife, a hip bag, and a handkerchief that had been purchased at Ogikubo Station (which could be reached directly from the station closest to the Miyazawa's house). Other items, such as a hat, gloves, and scarf were sold in the area around Atsugi Station. Police were able to track down a store in Atsugi that had sold three sweatshirts of the same brand discovered in the Miyazawa's house, and other stores along the same train line sold the same hip bags and handkerchiefs that were also found in the house.

The killer left his sweatshirt neatly folded on the second floor, covered in the splattered blood of his victims. It was size L (height 175 to 185 centimetres), manufactured in August 2000, and sold from September to November of the same year. The body of the sweatshirt was grey while the sleeves and area around the neck were purple, yet it had been washed numerous times and the colours had faded.

Specks of red optical brighteners (often used in laundry detergents) were discovered on the chest of the sweatshirt, in addition to other dyes and oils used in styrofoam for stage play sets. These were later discovered on the hip bag as well. Only 130 of the same sweatshirt were sold nationwide, and of those, only 10 across four stores in the Tokyo area. Police were only able to track down one of those sales, and the other nine still remain a mystery.

Police also found the killer's down jacket, neatly folded like the sweatshirt. It was a black Uniqlo jacket that went on sale in October 2000 and quickly sold out. Specks of the killer's own blood were found on the sleeves. In the pockets they discovered sand from Miura Peninsula (Kanagawa Prefecture, to the south of Tokyo) as well as dried leaves from weeping willows believed to be common along the water. They also discovered faeces that likely belonged to a small bird such as a sparrow. The Miyazawa family had stayed in a hotel on the Miura Peninsula two years before the murders, but police were unable to determine if there was any connection or if it was just a coincidence.

From footprints left in the house, police were able to determine the killer wore size 27.5 Slazenger tennis shoes made in South Korea between October 1998 and November 2000. They were unable to determine whether the man had imported them or bought them in Korea himself.

The killer also left behind a crusher hat (available for sale at the same stores as the sweatshirt), and a small grid-patterned scarf which may or may not have been picked up at a cheap 100 yen store. The scarf was only 130 centimetres long and considered too short for a full-grown adult to comfortably wear. Combined with the hip bag, police considered that the killer could have been a student still in his teens, but nothing was ever conclusively proven.

The sashimi knife was 34 centimetres long, with a blade 21 centimetres in length. It was one of 1,500 produced in Fukui Prefecture in June of that year. These knives were sold all around Tokyo, but the day before the murders a supermarket in Kichijouji, Musashino City (northwest of Setagaya) reported selling a sashimi knife to a man in his 30s wearing a black down jacket. He was roughly 170 centimetres tall, matching the description of the man on the train.

Two black handkerchiefs were discovered at the scene, 45 centimetre long types sold at Muji. There was a three centimetre cut in the middle of one; police believed the handkerchief was used on the handle of the sashimi knife to keep a firm grip in the face of blood splatter. The other handkerchief was folded into a triangle, and police believe the killer used it as a mask. The handkerchiefs were full of holes and also covered in the killer's blood, so it's possible he also tried to use them to stop his own bleeding. Police believed there to be some significance behind the killer wrapping his knife in this manner, and found that hunters, soldiers, and gang members in the Philippines did the exact same thing with their knives. Later evidence would lead the police to suspect the killer wasn't fully Japanese.

The hip bag found at the scene was one of 2,850 made in Osaka from 1995 to 1999. It was old and worn out, indicating the killer had likely been using it for a long time. It also had numerous cuts from a sharp object, and police discovered a special detergent on the outside that is used in cleaning off hard water; a detergent not often seen in Japan. Police suspected the killer frequently travelled overseas. They also found the same dyes on the sweatshirt both in and outside the bag, but further testing revealed that they likely came from a fluorescent highlighter; the type often used by school children. It was possible that during the 1995 to 1999 period the bag was on sale that the killer was still a student, placing him in his late teens or early 20s at the time of the murders.

Inside the bag they also found sand they believed came from Edwards Air Force Base in California. It matched the characteristics of sand located in the eastern part of the base. They also discovered the same sand from Miura Peninsula as that found in the jacket. With California being the home of skateboarding, and Miura Peninsula also being popular with skateboarders, police believed that the killer may have had a strong interest in the sport. However, it should be noted that when the killer used the stairs in the Miyazawa home to go down to the first floor, he went down sideways with his back pressed to the wall; a method of movement used by trained soldiers. He did the same when moving around the bunk beds on the second floor.

By this point, you may have noticed many similarities that ultimately don't add up. Dyes on the killer's clothes were the same as those used on stage props, and he visited a popular theatre group website on the family's computer. The killer appeared to be well travelled and used techniques common in the Philippines, had sand from a Californian army base in his pockets, and descended the stairs in a trained military style. Yet the scarf and hip bag potentially belonged to someone who was a student or freshly graduated; someone younger than the man in his 30s seen on the train and buying the sashimi knife. This last point could be explained away; a short scarf proves very little and the man might have used highlighters for things other than school work, but it's harder to ignore the other points, particularly the potential military training and overseas travel.

After spending up to 11 hours in the Miyazawa's house, the killer left with 200,000 yen (Yasuko's cram school tuition fees). The father's sweatshirt was also missing, indicating the killer may have taken that after his own was bloodied. He left behind all the family's credit cards and didn't touch anything else. For a while it was thought the killer ran off with the family's New Year's cards when they couldn't be found, but it was later discovered that an officer had taken them as potential evidence and then forgotten to turn them back in. An envelope on the first floor bookshelf with 60,000 yen remained untouched.

Police performed DNA analysis on the criminal's blood and discovered maternal DNA indicating a European ancestor on his mother's side (particularly from the Mediterranean region), while paternal DNA indicated a father of East Asian descent. His mother may not have been European herself, but she may have had a European parent or grandparent. Analysis of the Y-chromosome revealed Haplogroup O-M122, a common haplogroup in East Asian peoples showing up in 1 in 5 Koreans, 1 in 10 Chinese, and 1 in 33 Japanese. This led investigators to seek help from INTERPOL, as the killer may not have been Japanese.

The police knew for sure that the killer was a male with type A blood. No drugs or alcohol were detected in his system, nor was he a smoker. He was most likely right handed, and judging by his clothes, around 170 centimetres tall. The length of the belt on his hip bag indicated the man had a slim build. They believed him to be between 15- to 35-years-old based on the evidence left behind and the physicality required to enter the house through the second-floor bathroom window. A man matching his description was seen buying a sashimi knife the day before the murders, and the afternoon following, another man matching the same description was seen on an express train out of Tokyo with a deep wound to his hand. Were these the same man? Police still don't know.

Almost half a million investigators worked on the case, making it one of the largest in Japanese history. The brutal nature of the crime—especially towards such young children—and the brazen disregard showed by the killer in the hours following sent the public and media into an uproar. The statute of limitations for the crime would have expired in 2015, letting the killer run free and never having to fear punishment for the four brutal murders ever again. Public outrage over the case saw the statute of limitations finally abolished in 2010, meaning the case remains open to this day. Numerous investigators still work full time on the case, and there is a 20 million yen reward for information leading to the killer's capture. As of this book's publication, police are still releasing new evidence to the media from the murders, and the crime remains fresh in the public's mind. The Miyazawa house remains abandoned, and officers visit it yearly to pay their respects.

Police are still unsure why the killer murdered the Miyazawa family. It may have been a burglary, considering he ran off with Yasuko's cram school tuition fees, but he left other money in the house untouched, didn't take any of the family's credit cards, and it doesn't explain why he so brutally murdered everyone either. The violent nature of the attack, in addition to the killer's movements throughout the house, indicated a man with military and/or gang experience. DNA indicated he may not have been Japanese, and evidence suggested the man was well-travelled. He left his blood, saliva, and fingerprints all over the house because he had no previous records for the police to compare to. Who was this man, and why did he brutally murder an entire family the night before New Year's Eve?

Investigations are still ongoing, and family members of the deceased still take to the streets to distribute leaflets on the anniversary of the crime. Despite the massive amount of evidence left behind by the killer, police were unable to quickly solve the murders, but the horrific nature of it *did* propel the country to abolish its statute of limitations for murder. Police, family members, and the public continue to pray that the case will be solved soon and the vicious murderer brought to justice.

SOURCES

The following is a list of websites visited while gathering information for this book.

Abema Times: https://times.abema.tv/
Alphapolis: https://www.alphapolis.co.jp/
Asagei: https://www.asagei.com/
Asahi Shimbun Digital: https://www.asahi.com/
Bukimi Dick: https://bukimidick.com/
Business Career Online: https://business-career.jp/
Candy: https://candy-web.net/
Carat Woman: https://career-find.jp/
Chukyo TV News: https://www2.ctv.co.jp/news/
Dokujyo Channel: http://dokujyoch.net/
Dorosuki: http://www.wikihouse.com/dorosuki
Entertainment Topics: https://entertainment-topics.jp/
Excite News: https://www.excite.co.jp/news/
Imomushi no Yuutsu: https://imomushino-yuutu.com/
J-Cast News: https://www.j-cast.com/
Japan Today: https://japantoday.com/
Jiji Press: https://www.jiji.com/
Kowai Hanashi Net: https://kowaiohanasi.net/
Matomedia: https://newsmatomedia.com/
Metropolitan Police Department: https://www.keishicho.metro.tokyo.jp/
Middle Edge: https://middle-edge.jp/
Mikaiketsu Jiken: https://seesaawiki.jp/w/mikaiketsujiken/
Missing Person Search: http://www.mps.or.jp/
Mukashi no News: http://mogx2.blog91.fc2.com/
National Police Agency: https://www.npa.go.jp/
Net no Chikara de: http://netpower1.blog14.fc2.com/
Nippon TV: http://www.ntv.co.jp/
Rakuten Infoseek: https://news.infoseek.co.jp/
Sankei News: https://www.sankei.com/

Tantei File: http://www.tanteifile.com/
The Mystery Taiken: http://kowasugiru.blog.jp/
The Tsuburu: https://sumaapu0.hateblo.jp/
Toyo Keizai Online: https://toyokeizai.net/
Uncleared Crimes: http://niconice.blog17.fc2.com/
Wikipedia: https://ja.wikipedia.org/
Windy: https://windy-windy.net/
Wotake no Jikenbo: http://jiken.crap.jp/
Yabusaka: http://yabusaka.moo.jp/
Yomiuri Online: https://www.yomiuri.co.jp/
Z-Files: http://occult.wp-x.jp/
Zakkan: https://ameblo.jp/maeba28/
Zawazawa: https://zawazawa.jp/

WANT EVEN MORE JAPANESE HORROR?

Read a sample from *Toshiden: Exploring Japanese Urban Legends*, also by Tara A. Devlin.

Sugisawa Village

Hidden deep within the mountains of Aomori Prefecture there exists a village called Sugisawa. One day, a man from the village went crazy. Within a single day he killed everyone living in the village and then took his own life.

Nobody knows why he went crazy, nor why he went on such a violent crime spree. But the end result of this horrific crime remained the same: Sugisawa Village became empty.

The events of that day were so cruel that the local government decided to leave the village abandoned, and at the same time deny anything ever took place. They then erased all trace of the village from the local maps.

Luckily the village was deep in the mountains, so it was easy to cover the events up. But, of course, they couldn't erase the fact that the horrific crime *did* take place in the first place.

There were rumours of thick bloodstains all over the village, and those who approached the village would undoubtedly be cursed by the evil spirits that lived there.

Furthermore, according to the legend, it's

impossible to reach Sugisawa unless you leave the straight path that leads further into the mountains. Then you will find a sign with a warning standing at the entrance. That sign states "You may enter, but do so at your own risk."

You can also find an old red shrine gate at the entrance, and a stone shaped like a skull sitting at its feet.

ABOUT

The legend of Sugisawa Village first appeared in the 1990s, although the events mentioned in the legend itself are purported to take place early in the Showa era (the late 1920s and early 30s). The story was one of the first and biggest to be spread through the internet in a time when it was just starting to take off. The story became so popular that several media outlets picked up on it, and it was through the TV show *Kiseki Taiken Unbelievable* in 2000 that it truly reached the masses. The episode set out to find this fabled village and determine whether it actually existed or not. They searched throughout not just Aomori Prefecture but similar stories all over Japan, but in the end they never found it. The program then claimed that Sugisawa Village must exist in a space-time warp, able to appear and disappear at will. After the program aired many people set out to find the village themselves, uploading blog entries and later YouTube videos on their findings, many of which you can still watch on the internet today. Despite claims to the contrary, nobody has ever found the "real" Sugisawa Village of legend, and it's unlikely anyone ever will.

HISTORY

The legend of Sugisawa Village began in Aomori, the place the village is supposed to be located. There was a real village call Kosugi. It was a small village in the Obatakezawa district of Aomori City. This area received its name because of "a mountain stream that flows through the cedar forest." *Sugi* means cedar and *sawa* means marsh or mountain stream. People would say they were going to "the cedar," which sounded a lot like the word "Sugisawa" in Japanese, and thus it came to be affectionately called that. However, the village was only accessible by foot, and as the years passed it became abandoned because of depopulation, not a murderous crime spree. So how did the benign village of Sugisawa become the fabled site of such a horrific crime?

There was an actual crime in 1938, the same time the Sugisawa legend is supposed to have happened, that took place in the small village of Kamo, close to Tsuyama in Okayama Prefecture. A man, Mutsuo Toi (21 at the time) killed 30 people and injured three before killing himself. Toi had tuberculosis, and in his suicide note claimed that the villagers treated him cruelly, so he wished to extract revenge. He snuck into people's homes over the course of a single night and using a shotgun, katana, and axe, killed over half the village's occupants before killing himself at dawn. Although Okayama and Aomori are separated by quite a distance, somehow the story of this crime in Okayama was adapted to the abandoned village in Aomori and became the modern day legend of Sugisawa Village.

There exist even more crazy rumours about the truth of Sugisawa. Some claim it's actually a cover-up for a secret government Echelon base, while others have claimed it's a settlement for old Templar Knights. Apparently you can find Jesus Christ's grave in Aomori Prefecture as well. Who knew?

FINDING THE VILLAGE

There are several key signs that you have stumbled upon Sugisawa Village:

- There is a sign at the entrance that states "You must not proceed past this point. There can be no guarantee for your life if you do." There are variations on the exact wording, but in every version the sign states that if you go past it, you will be in big trouble.
- There is an old, red shrine gate at the entrance to the village, beneath which you'll find a stone shaped like a skull.
- Upon entering the village you'll find several abandoned buildings with bloodstains on the walls.

WITNESS'S ACCOUNTS

There are several creepypastas on the internet from

people who claim to have visited Sugisawa. The following is a common tale shared amongst friends of friends:

One day, two young men and a woman went for a drive deep in the mountains when they got lost and stumbled upon an old, beat up shrine gate. Beneath the gate there were two large stones, one of them shaped like a skull.

The young driver saw it and remembered a rumour he'd heard long ago. The rumour was that a skull found at the bottom of a shrine gate was a sign of the entrance to Sugisawa.

The two men got out of the car; however, the young woman said to them, "I'm scared, let's get out of here." They decided to search the village, however, and all went in together.

About 100 metres after passing under the shrine gate, they suddenly found a large open area before them with four old, abandoned buildings. The three of them stepped inside one of the buildings and inside they found a large amount of dried blood on the walls.

The two men felt a shiver run up their spines, and the woman suddenly cried out.

"Hey, there's something strange about this place. I can feel a presence!"

The three of them fled the building in surprise, and as they did, they felt like they were being surrounded by a large number of people.

The three of them ran for the car. However, something was wrong. No matter how much they ran they couldn't seem to reach the car.

The open space to the car should have only been 100 metres, and it was a straight path so there's no way they could have gotten lost. Even so, as the three of them kept running and running they couldn't escape from Sugisawa.

Unawares, the woman suddenly found herself separated from the two men, and as she kept running for what felt like forever she somehow finally found herself back at the car. Thankfully, the keys were still in the ignition. She climbed into the driver's seat to go and get help and turned the key to start the car.

However, no matter how much she turned the key the car refused to start. On the verge of tears she kept turning the key, over and over, trying to get the car to go.

Then…

Don don don.

A large sound suddenly reverberated from the windscreen. She looked and noticed the windscreen was covered in bloody red handprints.

No, not just the windscreen. Countless bloody red handprints appeared on all the windows as though they were all being beat upon at the same time.

The woman crouched down in fear, and before long she fainted…

The next morning one of the locals, out for a morning walk, stumbled upon the bloody car and the dumbfounded young woman inside. Her hair had turned white from fear overnight.

She was taken to the hospital where she explained her terrifying experience. Afterwards she disappeared and was never seen again. Her two male friends were also never found.

The following is a tale from someone calling themselves Matsu-san:

This is a story someone who went to Sugisawa Village told me. They were driving up the mountain when they finally found a gravel road they could pass through when they found a sign. They ignored it and kept going before they realised they'd arrived at Sugisawa Village. The place apparently stank of garbage.

There were a few wooden buildings and a lot of rubbish lying around. This person felt someone watching them, though, and feeling creeped out they left. A few days later a friend who was with the person at the time died.

And the following is from Keiko-san in Saitama:

I went to Aomori Prefecture to go mountain climbing. About two hours into climbing the area was wrapped in fog, and I couldn't see well. I made my way slowly up the mountain so I didn't fall and there were several villages along the way.

Then it was like there was this village smack bang in the middle of the jungle. It was dark, so I pulled out my torch and approached it. There were six buildings in total, and I went from house to house checking each one. There was no sign that anybody lived there. All I saw were two cats.

While I was walking around, I sensed somebody

approaching me, yet when I looked around nobody was there. It was incredibly strange.

There were houses further back in the village as well, but I was too scared to go and look at them. About 20 minutes later I noticed a man standing behind me. He was wearing a straw hat and had pale skin and blue eyes. I said hello, but he said nothing in reply. I paid him no attention and kept walking, but then he suddenly screamed and ran at me.

I ran and finally reached the sign that stated I was back on the mountain climbing track. That was the first time I'd ever been so scared. I still don't know what that guy was doing there now. I told people about what happened there, but nobody believes me.

The following message was posted by someone claiming to be a police officer in Aomori:

Sugisawa Village exists. It's close to Aomori Airport…

But you must never go looking for it, and please don't enter it half-cocked.

Because if you do, you'll never come back…

WANT EVEN MORE?

Also available in *Kowabana: 'True' Japanese scary stories from around the internet*:
Volume One
Volume Two
Volume Three
Origins
Volume Five

Aokigahara: The Truth Behind Japan's Suicide Forest

Toshiden: Exploring Japanese Urban Legends
Volume One
Volume Two

Reikan: The most haunted locations in Japan

The Torihada Files:
Kage
Jukai
Kirei
Kazoku

Read new stories each week at Kowabana.net, or get them delivered straight to your ear-buds with the *Kowabana* podcast!

ABOUT THE AUTHOR

Tara A. Devlin studied Japanese at the University of Queensland before moving to Japan in 2005. She lived in Matsue, the birthplace of Japanese ghost stories, for 10 years, where her love for Japanese horror really grew. And with Izumo, the birthplace of Japanese mythology, just a stone's throw away, she was never too far from the mysterious. You can find her collection of horror and fantasy writings at taraadevlin.com and translations of Japanese horror at kowabana.net.